DANCING THROUGH A DELUGE

First published in Great Britain 2024 by Mirador Publishing

Copyright 2024 by Jess Wells
Cover design by pisky.co.uk

First edition: 2024

Any reference to real names and places is purely fictional and are constructs of the author. Any offense the references produce is unintentional and in no way reflects the reality of any locations or people involved.

A copy of this work is available through the British Library.

ISBN: 978-1-917411-06-6

Mirador Publishing
7 Cossington Lane
Woolavington
Somerset
UK
TA7 8HL

Visit our website at www.jesswells.com

Dancing Through a Deluge

Jess Wells

"**Jess Wells has cleverly reimagined the world through the eyes of an unlikely heroine,** a tiny, misshapen former nun wandering the countryside. In a case of mistaken identity, she finds herself in charge of an estate and the lives of **a colorful cast of characters,** each grappling with their identities, past demons, and hopes for the future. **This captivating story will restore your faith in human nature and the ability to rise from the depths of despair to reinvent a future in an entirely new landscape**. Heroes and villains abound but the irrepressible human spirit restores our faith in humanity. **A clever, poignant, uplifting read**." - Catherine Hemingway, author of *The Matchmaker of Pemberley*.

"Few have the ability to take a moment in time past and render it fully with sights, sounds, odors and emotions. Jess Wells has it and her latest, *Dancing Through a Deluge*, is **a delightful example of a story—part fable, part legend—where you can not only enjoy the 14th century cast of characters but also identify with them, many centuries later**." - Felice Picano, author of *Pursuit: A Victorian Entertainment*

Dancing Through a Deluge by Jess Wells is a smile-inducing tale of danger and delight… **a riveting and immersive story that blurs the lines between the wretched and the righteous. Magnificent character development** is showcased by a cast of individuals such as MT, Claudia, Percy, Jacob, and more. … **A carefully measured pace that intensifies as**

the pages turn results in an exemplary read for fans of novels with a historical setting. I can easily recommend this novel with a wink and a smile. - Gaius Konstantine for *Readers' Favorite*

Dedicated to Evan, beloved son

CONTENTS

CHAPTER ONE

East Anglia, England, 1351

Sister Mary Thomas didn't really mind that she was frequently mistaken for a bear.

She had spent a year and a half trudging the length of England, then to the northern tip of Scotland and back south to Thetford east of York. During eight months of that journey, she had lived under a huge bearskin pelt that completely covered her and the little cart she was pulling. She was very short and tremendously wide, shaped like a gourd, a mere four feet tall when the average man was more than five. The long brown arms of the pelt hung to the ground where the bear's shiny black claws clacked on pebbles and stones, and because the front of the bearskin pelt was nailed to posts on the cart like an awning, she could walk protected from wind and rain, completely unseen. Its rich brown fur shone in the sun of the Scottish dales, glistened among the trees in Northumberland where she plodded. Like a bear.

As a nun she had been assigned to grow and burn sage to

purify the air, so she had hung a censer to swing in front of the cart, and it made her look like a bear belching smoke.

She didn't mind: hiding under the pelt kept the wolves at bay. Dogs who were now homeless and emboldened rerouted their hunt to avoid her. Horses and sheep, who had never seen a bear, somehow knew enough to shy away and while she regretted that she frightened the does and fawns, pheasants and chicks, at least it kept people away.

The first people who saw her initially stopped in awe, since wild bears hadn't been seen in England for more than 300 years. Then they fled crying, as if they had had enough courage to survive the recent death of every second person in the world from an invisible and unknown disease, but to witness the arrival of an animal from myth and legend was a bridge too far. Thankfully, she was shunned by needy people. By the heartbroken and frantic. The disillusioned and confused. Sick people. Those she had tried to help avoid death but who had died anyway. With a gasping breath, they died as they fled their looms and homes. They died behind the plow, at the butter churn, in the chicken coops, on their knees in church.

Even before she had the bearskin pelt, she had leaned into the crossbar of the cart and trudged north past hamlet after village as if she were seeking the boundary of the contagion. She paused at a gathering of people praying on their knees in the square, fervent and disciplined, and yet still falling over dead. She didn't join them, though as the only member of the clergy she had seen in days she could have led their prayers.

Instead, she plodded on, as if foot in front of foot was the only logic she could find, and in the following week came upon a hamlet holding a week-long, drunken bacchanal, with all the ale casks open, two pigs on the spit, everyone dancing and singing and flinging their arms around with abandon. Good fabric wasted on bad costumes; bedding pulled into puddles. They were in rebellion against the church's admonitions, in rebellion against the careful pairing of the miller's son and the baker's daughter, the advantageous, the strategic, the well planned. Rebelling even against the romantic, for what is love in the face of putrefaction, what is compatibility and devotion when most will be dead by morning? The only question for them was 'what do you want most in this moment?' And their answer was to eat more than they could stomach, drink more than their brain could hold, and have sex until their bodies said quit.

Her trudging was rebellion as well: as a nun, she should sacrifice herself for the betterment of others, administer last rites whether they wanted it or not, but she had seen too much. She and her cart stayed on the outskirts of the party, although she did allow herself to revel in the laughter and song, baskets and bowls overflowing, the jig, the prance, the joke. Gallows humor is still humor, after all.

In the morning, she hurried away from the corpses and the broken crockery strewn by the cold fire.

It was The Great Mortality, or the Plague, which in this first wave was entirely respiratory and therefore invisible; more contagious, fast-acting and lethal than the waves of plague that would follow. Half of mainland Europe died. Forty percent of England!

The remaining people in England, like dice in a cup, had been shaken and scattered to unknown corners and surprising new identities. They were unable to tell if they had survived through grace, luck, atonement, a refusal to approach the docksides, a refusal to approach the cities, or the shunning of company altogether. They seemed to have abandoned morality as well, stealing what they had coveted from their neighbor, ransacking homes in their path as they ran, panicked, toward an unknown destination.

Now that she had trodden north, south and so far east that Sister Mary Thomas was just a week away from the North Sea, it had become remarkably quiet. The dying had stopped, and the corpses and carrion were buried, consumed, or hidden in the weeds. But things were still not normal. She trod down what were now deserted roads so silent that they made her feel she must be late to chapel or hadn't been invited to the party. Now there was no one in the fields, no markets or farmer's wagon, no shepherd or hunters or girls picking fruit. No sickle or thresher, whip, rake or broom. Just a quiet forest. Wind in the trees. Birds in the brush.

Today, Sister Mary Thomas, or MT as she called herself now, strained against the weight of the cart. It was late in the afternoon, time to decide on shelter for the night and she was certain that she had seen ribbons floating a few feet above the ground on a hillock in the distance. They looked new or at least tended to, not trampled or torn. Oddly festive. And to the east of them a mill and a farm, halfway up the hill a manor house, and at the crest, a tall stone lodge of a rabbit warren. She reasoned that it was as good a place to stay as any: there might be eggs from feral chickens, but it was really the ribbons that drew her on. Who, she wondered, had held onto gaiety in the midst of all this?

She passed the silent mill without pausing but stopped in front of a roadside chapel that she hadn't seen. Its outdoor altar to Mother Mary was stuffed with leaves while ivy had grown over her stone face and down her faded blue dress. MT set down the cart and stepped out from under the pelt, stretched her shoulders and scraped at the leaves on the statue to stop the blasphemy of nature and neglect, then fiddled with the latch on the door, put her shoulder into it and burst into the chapel.

Her attendance to the statue felt odd to her: she had given up her wimple months ago and her hair that had grown back patchy and wild, swirling in cowlicks that had been shaven for so many years that she had forgotten she had them. Several times a day now, she ran her hands over her neck, through her hair, a sensual delight that she had never experienced. It was a yardstick for how far she had come, more indicative than how tattered and stained her black habit was or her formerly white collar that was now just a tab of soiled cloth at the nape of her neck.

In the chapel, Sister MT ran her hands along the arm rests of the pews, across the empty altar that no longer held whatever measly candlesticks or cups had been on top. Even the floor had been violated – chipped at with chisels and hammers to free a collection of small millstones that had been cemented into the floor. MT regarded them quizzically: most millstones were enormous and were kept in the mill that was controlled by the bishop or lord of the manor. Peasants grow the grain, and the lord gets a cut. Peasants grind the grain, and the bishop gets a cut. In most villages, even the communal oven was owned by a royal. These millstones, however, were cottage-sized, peasant-sized, a violation of the bishop's monopoly, and she could just imagine a sheriff riding hut to hut and confiscating them, turning them over to the bishop who had them cemented into the floor as a reminder to everyone who knelt there in prayer that the bishop would not be usurped, that rebellion was futile.

But the millstones also made her think of bread, which reminded her that she was hungry, and that there might be food in the manor house.

She rolled back the bearskin and took inventory of what little food she had, then strode with purpose, knocked on the door, announced herself when she pushed it open. But she saw the tell-tale signs of another ransacked home: faded spots on the wall from wood carvings and tapestries long gone, cupboard doors nearly torn off their hinges, fine furniture smashed and half-stuck into fireplaces for kindling. It didn't bode well but she persisted as her stomach growled. She headed to the kitchen.

A stripped larder, empty flour bin, a bit of moldy bread she left for the mice. But her small stature rewarded her: the very back of a low cupboard in the pantry yielded a smoked ham and a jug of wine. She dragged them out, lifted the ham to the table and climbed onto a stool as she pulled a knife from her belt. She cut slices then chunks of the meat and ate with abandon. The jug of wine she left on the floor. Had never touched the stuff other than in church. But the world was ending, that had been clear, even now that the dying had stopped. As she had discarded her wimple and rebelled against her religion, her sobriety had lost its meaning today. She uncorked the jug, took a small sip, then a gulp, feeling a warmth course through her, and right behind it, the softening of intent, the dulling of the sharp edge of life. It all seemed more manageable, of less importance. She left the ham in the kitchen but carried the jug, swigging from it as she wandered through the house, flinging open doors with increasing bravado and sighing over the beds that had been stripped of fabric and the curtains that hung ragged and slit.

In a library most of the shelves were empty but in the middle of the room there was a heavy, commanding desk, made of dark wood with ornate carvings. Surprisingly, there were stairs next to the desk that led up to a chair, as if to help a child. MT staggered the length of the room, her hand bracing her as it ran across wood paneling that was usually found only in great halls, castles, and cathedrals. At the final panel, she leaned against the wall and as she pushed herself off to investigate the desk, a panel sprung open in the wall to reveal a closet.

Hung inside the closet panel was a horizontal rack with three hat forms but it held only two skull caps, one black, one white, the kind a woman would wear to bed or a man under a metal helmet. Unlike the usual simple caps, these were richly embroidered all the way down to the ear flaps. They were covered with small shards of reflective glass amid a scene of lions killing an elk. On the closet door hung a mirror at exactly MT's height, which surprised her, and next to it hung a portrait of a ferocious looking woman with a mole on her chin in a fine dress wearing the white cap. Odd that she would wear this cap instead of a hat with plumes or jewels, MT thought. The woman in the portrait rested her hand on the back of a shaggy, grey elkhound that was so close to her height that the dog looked as big as a pony. MT took the black cap off its stand and tried it on. It fit her unusually small head and short neck. Looking in the mirror she didn't recognize herself, as if her face had been swallowed up by the needlework and sparkle of the cap. Colors inside the closet caught her eye: dresses hung at the right height for a child – or for her, MT chortled drunkenly – as she held one up to her, then struggled out of her habit and tried on the dress. It fit as well as the cap had. As if it had been tailored for her. It fit the precise curve of her wide hips, the length of her shortened arms, the outline of her little breasts.

What were the chances, she laughed, that after a lifetime of being treated like a freak she would find another woman just her stunted height and spreading width? Her odd shape had been the impetus for ridicule and jokes her whole life: the nuns had claimed it was almost impossible to tailor a habit the length of a man's shirt and the width of a mule's behind. As a young novice she had cried at night over their cruelty but as a young woman whose job was growing, drying and burning sage in the censer, she blew smoke up into their faces when they stared down at her and pushed them aside with the heel of her hand on the mound between their hips. It stunned them and the shock of being touched in such a place kept them from reporting her to the Abbess.

Today in the empty manor house, MT smoothed the front of a festive aquamarine dress made from finer fabric than she had ever worn, with satin laces and rabbit fur on a low-cut neckline. In what world could she live like this woman did? Four dresses in the closet and empty boxes for four more: a wealthy woman. She twirled unevenly across the room, marveling over clothing that actually fit her. She straightened the cap and, holding her skirt up like a lady, she mounted the stairs to the desk chair.

"Plant the fields by sundown," she drunkenly ordered invisible servants and slammed her palm on the desktop. "Butcher a pig for the banquet. And then…draw me a bath!"

She threw her head back to laugh and as she did, her foot hit a lever that was high above the floor on the underside of the desk. Another hidden door opened, and an over-filled bag spilled gold coins in a puddle beneath her feet. More riches than she had ever seen. A forgotten fortune. Undiscovered by marauders whose feet would hang far too low to touch the lever or noticed by thieves who had taken even the hinges from doors in the other rooms. A trick of the drink, she reasoned, as she laid her head on her arm and passed out.

A tremulous voice woke MT several hours later. "I said… we are all so grateful that you have returned to us, Baroness."

MT, only half-way into the dress, jerked awake and wiped the spittle from her face.

A slim but muscular peasant in a knit cap stood in front of the desk, his head bowed, and his hands raised, offering two gutted, skinned rabbits.

Looking down at the expanse of skin she was exposing, she was horrified. She shrugged the dress higher onto her shoulders and pulled at the side laces. She had no idea how to fasten a dress like this but hiked it up in front and tied the laces as best she could. The cap, askew now, still covered her hair. Returning from the soft world of wine was more difficult than she had imagined.

The man tried to bow even lower. "Shall I fetch enough to feed the sheriff, milady?"

"Sheriff?"

She heard heavy boots in the hall. Her black habit lay like a rag in front of the open closet with its portrait and mirror. The gold coins pooled under the desk and prevented her efforts to quickly close the hidden door with her foot. The sheriff? She could be charged with theft but even more dangerous, she could be imprisoned for impersonating a royal. Just the misuse of a name or the possession of a cape of a forbidden color could have you pelted with old fruit in the stocks at best, sometimes locked up, even strung up.

The sheriff burst into the room. "Baroness," he said and bowed stiffly.

MT cleared her throat, straightened her back. Could she laugh off her appearance as a lark? Drunken excess? To the kitchen help, perhaps, but not a sheriff. She looked down at her hands and saw that she clutched three of the gold coins. Not her money. Not her station.

He averted his eyes. "Your...delivery... has arrived, milady."

MT reasoned that there was no way back, only forward,

and reassured herself that the charade only had to hold until the sheriff left. She could do that, couldn't she? She would take delivery of whatever it was and send him on his way. MT assumed a superior manner, stepped carefully down the stairs, grunted and waved him on. She checked for signs of contagion then stepped close to him: their disparate height meant that he would have to bend double if he wanted to look in her eyes. He obviously knew the baroness and especially with the portrait of the woman hanging on the cabinet door for comparison, he might see that despite the surprising similarity in their shape and size, she wasn't the baroness.

"You, there!" She barked at the young man with the rabbits, though it pained her to be so sharp. "Stand outside the door and refuse entry to anyone except me, is that clear?"

"Yes, milady. Take care, though. There's a bear outside the chapel." He took his post as sentry, his back stiff against the doorframe, with the rabbits still dangling from his fists.

A bear, she thought. *Had he seen her arrive?*

"Please, milady," he said plaintively, stepping toward her, though he bowed his head again. He wore a simple vest with pockets and tabs for tools. He was tanned and trim.

"I will be... very careful of the bear. Thank you." *Odd young man*, she thought as he stepped back and resumed his position.

The sheriff looked away from her: the embroidered and mirrored cap reflected back a gnarled version of him. "We're putting them in the barn."

She silently walked down the hill beside the sheriff.

Baudwin Pierce was tall and thin, marked by scars on his hands and a left shoulder that didn't move as freely as the right. His black hair was tied back, his face had the pallor of old meat. His doublet hung loosely as if he had recently lost a lot of weight.

"So, you're home now," Baudwin said carefully. "Where have you been, if I may ask, milady."

She glowered at him, hoping it was an appropriate response.

"Sequestered and grieving." For the world, for someone in particular. Claiming grief was a safe enough bet these days. "Though no, you may not ask." A lady of her station would not be questioned by a sheriff.

Just a few minutes more and she could flee, she told herself, but when she entered the barn her breath caught in her throat. The sheriff's men were herding people into the shadowy interior of the barn. Prisoners. Women who were crying and men who were resisting. She heard women outside calling out names, pleading for help.

"Very wise to build the walls up to the ceiling," the sheriff said. "Several men are strong and may need... further persuading. There are so few people left to work the harvest that we're lucky we found these many, and the two deliveries prior."

The barn was actually a jail, she realized. Two prior deliveries? Several of the men looked like they'd been beaten, and they glared at her.

She was horrified by this woman she was pretending to be. Who would allow this? Who would build a prison on their own property? Or was this woman so weak that her husband could create this without her knowing or without her having any power to do anything about it? She was either a monster or an accomplice to a monster but since it was one of those, she couldn't act horrified or uninformed. At this point, if she was found out, she would wind up on the other side of the fencing beside the rest.

"And this gentle-…this man?" She pointed at a wizened and crippled man, huddling against the stall's front slats. "What…use is he?"

"We took the rest, so he'd starve otherwise. Left it to the baron to decide," the sheriff said.

The old man's eyes were at the same level as MT's, and leaning into his gaze, she asked him quietly. "Where are you from?"

"Just outside York."

"Have you ever been here before?"

"No milady, nor known anyone 'twas."

She turned away from him and questioned the sheriff. "Again, remind me of their crimes."

"Violating the Act of Laborers by asking double in wages. No one to work in the fields but this lot is being demanding and running off. The royals won't have it."

She turned before the sheriff could see her look of horror and then she spotted the largest cell, filled exclusively with women who were either crouching with toddlers or pushing themselves against the slats and pointing to the lane outside the barn. "Our girls, milady. Don't let them take our girls!"

MT hurried outside as a driver climbed into the seat of

another wagon where young women and girls pressed themselves against the rounds of the wooden bars, calling to her with outstretched hands.

"Where are these women going?" she barked.

The sheriff rocked on his heels and stuck his thumbs into his belt.

"To the bishop. Bawdy houses are empty like the rest of the country. You have... an arrangement I hear."

"Open it! Open it at once!" Her outrage overwhelmed her need for the charade. "How dare you try to make off with..." She paced the length of the wagon, considering her situation. "...those who should be my weaving staff, my kitchen help. Release these women at once!"

"Better money for all where they're going," the driver said as he shrugged and sucked his teeth.

"Open it!" she shouted. "Put them in...with the other women."

MT shuffled her feet and tried not to see the women as they were roughly put into the cell or the way they hugged each other at their reunion. She turned away from the rage on their faces that said she had been guilty of their capture.

"Milady, let me cook for you," a woman offered.

"Yes, yes," MT said, but turned away.

The sheriff stepped forward. "The bishop is expecting..."

"Then the bishop can arrive to discuss it. I have come home to find my house ravaged and all my servants gone! You think I care about his bawdy houses? I care about the sheriff hunting down the thieves who have stripped my home!"

Baudwin bowed his head quickly. "As you wish, milady.

Good of you to take them while we finish the jail." The sheriff mounted his horse.

A jail? How much worse could this get? "And the progress is?" MT asked with what she hoped was a demanding tone.

"We break ground tomorrow. I'll be taking the strongest men here with me in the morning. I'll leave four of my best men to watch the prisoners tonight. And to protect you, of course." He turned away again from the look of her cap. His men stood sentry outside the barn leaning on pikes, knives jutting from their belts.

MT considered her situation. If the baron or baroness had a part in starting the plan, she could stop it as well, couldn't she? But it had to be done quickly because the real lady and lord of the manor might show up: maybe there was time to free the prisoners, steal the gold, and be gone. Now she had another reason to be believable. After a year of pointless praying and false promises, she could finally do some good. She couldn't leave now. Not with all these people who needed her. And she was ashamed to say, with all the gold where she had left it.

"Take the men now," she said sharply. "And your sentries. I've no need of protection from a group of... undernourished women." She waved her hand dismissively. "Can't feed the men anyway. Save you the trip back to collect them."

"Very well," the sheriff said begrudgingly. Another night of hard tack and a bedroll. "We'll ride to the jail site now."

She turned away as the men were re-loaded into the carts and one of them spat on her shoes as he was strong-armed out of the barn. A real lady would have him punished, but MT did not want to bring attention to her tell-tale battered shoes.

The sentries bolted the doors on the carts but grumbled that the new plan would delay their dinner.

After they had gone, MT paced slowly into the darkness of the barn and gripped a slat of a corral to hide her trembling. It wouldn't do to let all these women in on her secret by just opening the gates and letting them run: any one of them could trade her freedom for theirs. Besides, the sheriff was still too close to the manor and would just imprison them again.

"I know you're not her," a voice whispered close to her ear.

MT shuddered but then held herself rigid.

"Let me help you," the woman said.

CHAPTER TWO

MT felt that it had been years since anyone had offered to help her. Her two jobs had been smudging the nunnery with sage to clean the air, and polishing the walls, pews, tables, statuary and doors. She knew about wood beetles, sun damage on oak, and when a sage crop was ready for harvest. As soon as the plague began though, the priest who ruled the order like a little king stuffed his bags with the church's silver plate and ran away. Monks disavowed their calling so quickly that it became common to see their brown robes cast off and rotting by the roadside. Her Mother Superior was given a solemn and tearful burial followed by two days of prayers until the nuns who tended the sick in town died after a night of bloody coughing. Too frightened to enter the convent even to sleep in her bed, MT decided to live in the nunnery's garden wrapped in her cape with a smudge stick of sage burning while she ate carrots and jammed pole beans into her mouth. Next to die were the novices who went into the village for bread.

MT dug graves for the nuns who fell in the pews and the kitchens, for women who spilled clean laundry on the stairs – one by one – until there was just a single nun other than her. When there was no sign of life in the nunnery for two days she still couldn't bring herself to go inside, even to retrieve and bury the last body. She hoped that praying from afar would be enough. She harvested the sage, first with her customary care for the leaves, then tearing the plants out frantically, loading them into the convent's small cart and heading north.

As there were nearly no priests left, the Pope had decreed that nuns could say mass, baptize, and perform last rites so MT was besieged on the road by mothers cradling their children and husbands begging her to come to their cottage. Save me, they said. Bless my wife. Shield my child. Relieve my grief. Explain this madness. They ran toward her, demanding. Give me comfort, the people said, ensure my way to heaven. All she could do was mumble prayers as she smudged herself and all the living she came across, purifying the air and their breath. When she kept a sage bundle burning in the censer on the post she had nailed to the cart, people followed the aromatic smoke trail to find her. Frightened by the press of them, she hauled the post out of its holder and used it as a pike to smudge them from a distance. As she headed north, she ate from gardens and chicken coops, dug out sage wherever she found it but wouldn't enter a building of any kind. With every mile she walked, she looked and felt less like a servant of God.

Then, even before she donned the bearskin pelt, no one ran to her any longer: either she had become so dirty and tattered that she didn't look like a nun, or death had been so efficient in sweeping through the countryside that there was no one left to beg for solace. She spent her days pushing her cart and digging graves for anyone she came across.

One day, after months alone with her cart, the corpse of another family littered the roadway and MT knew it was reprehensible to leave the children and their mother to be feasted on by wolves so after smudging herself and them, she started to dig a single grave for the three.

"Let me help you," a man called out as he stepped out of the forest. "Let me help you dig."

He wore a cloth over his mouth and nose, a hat low on his forehead and he gripped a cloth sack in one of his gloved hands while he tossed another bulging sack onto the road.

Warily, she drove the shovel into the ground and stepped over to her cart to stand behind the billowing sage.

He efficiently dug the grave but before he rolled the woman into the hole he checked her for jewelry, slipped a ring off her finger and put it in his pocket while turning a steely eye to MT. He tore a bit of lace off the little girl's dress but placed her body carefully on top of her mother.

"Where to next, Sister?" he asked, when he finished filling in the grave.

~ * ~ * ~ * ~

In the manor house barn that had been made a prison, MT tried not to hear the women huddled in the straw who were calling to her, but to concentrate on the offer of help and the threat of exposure. She clutched the slat of the corral and looked at a woman who was on her knees and so just at MT's level, a buxom woman with a baby strapped to her chest, her blonde hair braided and twisted in an elaborate puzzle.

"I lived here," the woman whispered. "My name is Claudia. You need to know the house. The fields."

MT looked down at her shoes. "Who else knows?"

"No one. They're all from the north."

"Why would you help me?"

The woman sputtered her reply. "Because you'll free me!" She held the baby closer to her.

"I won't be here long," MT said and turned to face the voluptuous woman.

Claudia reached into her pocket and with a smooth swipe, slashed the end of MT's chin with a small knife, then wiped the blade on the edge of the slat.

MT stepped back, horrified, as the blood pooled in her cupped hand.

"Oh, milady!" Claudia exclaimed, "you've snagged yourself on the wood! Let me help you." She stood up and motioned for MT to open the corral. Wide-eyed, MT unlocked the gate with shaking hands as the blood dripped off her chin, and the woman with the baby slipped out. MT locked the gate again as the other women surged forward.

"What have you done?" MT whispered to her.

"To explain the absence of the mole," she whispered as she bent to give MT a cloth for her bloody chin. She cupped MT's elbow and led her toward the house, the remaining women calling to them as they left.

Good thinking, MT realized. The lack of the mole. She

clearly was not equipped to pull off this dangerous charade even for an afternoon. They crossed the courtyard toward the house, MT pressing the cloth into her wound. "This is just temporary," MT whispered. "I have no intention of…"

"Even if it's for a single day, a single hour," Claudia said firmly, "you mustn't let the others see you fumbling in what should be your own home. You have twenty possible spies. Thirty if you count the children, which you should. They should all live here or leave here believing your story."

"Oh, Mother Mary, we'll be strung up, no doubt," MT said.

Claudia clutched the baby closer as a shiver went down her back. Why was she helping this woman? Punishment for assisting this impersonation would be cruel and would leave the baby an orphan. Why had she returned to this place? True, she had been brought here forcibly but why not just run down the hill and back into the forest? If there was anyone here who knew her, it would be disastrous. On the other hand, the resemblance between the baroness and this stranger was remarkable. The baroness had always had her clothing carefully tailored to follow the exact outline of her oddly shaped body. Even the cap fit perfectly on this woman who was the baroness's identical height. If she was a distant relation, even if she was illegitimate, this imposter could hold the key to her future, and the baby's.

Claudia described the manor under her breath, without gesturing or looking down at the cap. The well was in the back between the kitchen and bakery. High table and hearth upstairs of course. The baroness's bedroom through the library. Servants' quarters above the laundry. Porter's lodge between the main gate and the stables. A back gate, seldom used, at the south end of the kitchen gardens. Dovecote for fertilizer on the north side and, the source of much of the manor's wealth, a large rabbit warren with its lodge on the top of the hill.

"The warrener!" MT exclaimed but held her palm tightly against the slash on her chin. "He's standing guard outside the library, holding rabbits. Odd young man. Does he know the lady of the manor?"

Claudia thought carefully. The rabbit trade was men's business. The warrener worked with the lord, and she had never seen a young man even during the holiday feasts that included the Master of the Hounds, the Hawks, the Head of Stables, and the Warrener. They would have only seen the baroness from afar and the coincidence of MT's similar stature made detection unlikely. That was assuming that those men had survived the Great Mortality and might return.

Claudia stopped near the entrance to the house, took a step forward and turned so MT could see the entire length of her. Claudia turned away from the mirrored cap, as she had in the presence of the real baroness because she saw bits of a half-finished woman. She moved the baby to sit prominently on her linked arms, challenging this woman, so freakishly like the former lady of the manor, to react to the child. MT glanced beyond them to study the courtyard.

In the library, Claudia tended to MT's chin. "You should change your dress," she said. "This one is for a banquet."

Claudia returned to the barn to dispense water and calm the frightened women.

"All will eat tonight, fear not. You are safe now," she said as the women lunged toward the slats. "The Lady, in her generosity, will employ as many of you as she can." *Until we find a way to flee*, she should say, but the temporary nature of the set-up could not be revealed.

MT had insisted that each of the women be inspected and smudged with sage smoke. Claudia first smudged the room, then summoned each of the women individually. "Have you phlegm?" she asked. They had all arrived in the same cart, and none had fallen sick yet. *Perhaps the worst was over*, she thought, and crossed herself with hope.

"Tell me truly, who can cook? I hear that the place has been stripped so it will be a challenge to feed us all, but we'll see. Have we gardeners here? Any weavers? A baker? What about orphans: any child here alone?" One boy, tall for ten, stood up, and Claudia started assigning tasks to the others.

~ * ~ * ~ * ~

Jacob the warrener considered his post outside the library to be a great gift. He had never been inside the manor house and few things pleased him more than to be of service to the baroness. He was a simple man: his mother had died on the birthing bed and Jacob had arrived afterward, forcing his way into the world even when the midwife had given up, and the delay had robbed his intelligence. He grew up with such a kindly nature, though, that no one accused him of being the Devil's spawn. Women were drawn to him, to his glen green eyes, his cupid-bow mouth, the combination of a fit, manly body and a delicate, childish mind. His smile was quick and broad and had no guile or cynicism to it.

He had been given to the warrener and his barren wife, who were kind but distant, and he grew up tending the colonies of rabbits in pillow mounds, which are raised earth with tunnels underneath. The pillow mounds dotted the baron's vast estate, and the warrener described them to the baron by their cardinal positions relative to the manor house. But direction made no sense to Jacob, so the warrener had named the pillow mounds after the great queens of England. The first pillow mound and rabbit colony belonged to the ruling regent Queen Philippa of course. There was the den of Bertha of Kent; the small but complex mound of the Lady of the Mercians; the nearly abandoned colony of Matilda, queen for moments but still the Lady of the English; and the vast, spreading and well-constructed colony of Eleanor of Aquitaine. The warrener and Jacob tended crops for them and walked the expanse of the range – the coneygarth – from colony to colony, checking that the pillow mounds were protected from the wind by bushes; that the foxes and wolves hadn't crossed the deep gullies to lay siege to the rabbit's homes. They reinforced the tunnel openings with clay pipes or barrels and made sure the roofs were wide enough to protect the labyrinth within from rain. When he was old enough to walk the miles of the coneygarth alone, Jacob called out to the does for permission to approach and he made up rhymes for the rabbits, brought carrots from his bag and enticed them out so he could check their eyes and their teats. In the summer he would lie in the shade and cover himself with a special mixture he and the warrener had grown of timothy, brome and oat hay, so the rabbits would climb onto his body and munch.

Sometimes, the young maids of the village came across him while walking home or intentionally walked into the woods to find such a handsome, unspoiled man and they guided Jacob's hands across their breasts or down their skirts to another kind of mound. The fear of bearing a simpleton made the girls run away but it left the aroused Jacob understanding that his entire life was dedicated to females and their mounds.

In the manor library, Jacob snapped to attention and bowed again when MT entered. She thought there was something precious about this young man. Delicate. Alluring.

"I thank you for standing guard," she said. "Are there more rabbits in the warren?"

"We are quite overrun, milady." He had spent most of yesterday transferring does from the coneygarth of Eleanor to the queendom of Matilda and he feared they might be fighting.

"We have a household that is hungry so that is good news. What is your name, son?" *No, no,* she thought. *A nun would call him son, but a lady would not.*

He was surprised by the question. "Jacob, milady."

Would the baroness have known his name, she wondered as she registered his reaction. "Well, Jacob, you may have saved us. Saved us all." Again, kind like a nun, not haughty like a lady. "Take those to the kitchen and return with as many as Claudia demands."

"I will, milady. But… where is the kitchen?"

MT was heartened by his ignorance and tried to remember what Claudia had said. "Turn left at the bottom of the stairs."

MT locked the door to the library behind her and leaned on the door. By freeing the women, she had finally been someone's salvation. Twenty someone's. Thirty if you count the children which she should, she thought, and smiled at Claudia's wisdom. But just as the warm feeling came over her, she spied her tattered habit on the floor. She hurried to it, looking over her shoulder though the room was locked, balled it up and stuck it in the farthest corner of the closet. Claudia was right: a lady would not wear a dress like this at a time like this, she reasoned, as she stripped off her gown and donned a simpler dress, though it was still the finest fabric she had ever touched. There were tall stockings that warmed her feet, boots that fit surprisingly well, and a cape that was heavy and treated for rain.

The gold, though. Theft is a sin, she thought as she crawled under the desk and tried in vain to stuff the sack back behind the little door. She may have abandoned her religion, but she still had her morals. The bag wouldn't fit back inside. She fetched her dirty black dress and made a bundle for some of the gold, hiding it again in the closet. This wasn't theft, it was…reapportionment. She was just…storing it elsewhere. The door still would not latch. She poured more into her habit and with a shove of her shoulder, the door under the desk finally closed. She sat back on her haunches, hidden under the desk.

If she ran away now she might be forgiven for taking the relatively simple dress, especially if she left the rest of the gold behind. But the coins inside her habit marked her as a thief, and every moment she stayed she continued to impersonate a royal.

But she couldn't leave, with or without the gold, could she? How many more women were *en route*? There was good to be done here if she could free them all, and it surprised her that the idea brought her both solace and excitement. A chance to do good. She adjusted the odd cap on her head, straightened the portrait and mirror on the closet door which she left open so her resemblance to the baroness could be reinforced (though she hoped that she didn't look as wicked). She would stay just until it was safe to leave, she told herself, as she strode out to supervise the reconstruction of her cold and empty home.

As the newly freed women crossed the courtyard, MT sent three to the kitchens to scrounge for pans and start a fire; two of the strongest women to collect or cut wood. The youngest lass was to take the children and hunt for eggs in the shrubs. Two women turned on their heels and ran down the road, preferring their freedom to employment and MT had no intention of stopping them, though she worried that they would be recaptured by the sheriff. She sent four to dig or pick whatever had gone wild in the kitchen gardens. Three to search every room for any fabric of any kind that could be used for bedding. The rest were to follow her, she instructed, but they stood mesmerized by her cap, smiling as if a happy play was being acted out across it. She snapped her fingers to regain their attention and sent them to collect any tools they could find. It felt odd that they obeyed her without question, she thought. The old man was ushered to a stool by the cold kitchen hearth. MT sent the orphan boy down to the roadside chapel to bring up a cart that "she had seen while coming in," she said. She thought she saw pots and a few bowls in it, she feigned, and when it was retrieved she exclaimed over the bearskin pelt, ordering it taken into her bedchamber while fighting her desire to wrap the toddlers in it. She would take matters in hand herself, she thought tentatively, like a Mother Superior but without all the kneeling on cold stone.

Gertrude, who had been the most vocal when Claudia asked for a cook, had nearly sprinted up the hill and when MT opened the door she pushed ahead of the others. Any woman could offer to be the cook, and a lady wouldn't stand around to choose, so it was imperative that Gertrude take the position first. When she stood at the kitchen hearth, though, she threw up her hands in distress. Everything was gone. All the saucepans and skillets. There were no plates or bowls. There was a bent pan deep inside the long-unused firebox and the kitchen table wobbled as if someone had tried to pry off one of the legs. No food. No vessels. Even when a maid delivered the pots and ladles from the MT's cart, there weren't enough. How was she supposed to cook amid this wreckage? She would certainly be punished if the lady went hungry: any woman who would allow a prison built on her property was no friend. They had all put on grateful and humble faces when released from the cells, but they looked over their shoulders as they scurried through the manor. The house of a tyrant was a small step up from the jail they had been in. Especially a ransacked house.

Gertrude grabbed a young girl as she ran by and ordered her to collect the pan from the firebox. Gertrude, whose hair was the color of the copper pan, had started in kitchens at about the same age as this girl, and she had risen to second cook in a middling house in the west when the Angel of Death had swept through last year. The dying still lived in her mind as a sound. First the slosh and splat of a meat-filled trencher falling to the flagstones of the Great Room as the serving boy fell dead. Then the sound of well-padded ladies in waiting as they tumbled from the bench and wheezed on the floor; the jangle of plates and cups as the living disentangled themselves from the long tables to begin their fruitless run. She ran out the back with the young boy who tended her fires, and they had huddled together in the forest but in the morning he started to cough, and she leapt up and left him there, turning to see him stretch out his arm for her help.

She shook her head to dislodge the memory, as a girl brought a skirt full of eggs that she had plucked from under the bushes. Gertrude used a rag from her pocket to tie up her red hair and decided that it was just her luck: to be head cook amid devastation. The only question now was how to turn such a ramshackle place to her advantage?

CHAPTER THREE

It had been his pity for a horse that finally convinced Percy that he could improve his own lot in life.

He had been a lowly member of the baron's dog-tending team, answerable to the over-fed and social climbing Master of the Hounds and though Percy was lanky, blonde, muscled and lean, in the village even the maids called him the dog-boy. He wore the baron's colors and insignia but somehow everyone knew that he spent his days shoveling dog shit and it was fruitless to tell them that he was a skillful dog trainer, that puppies learned quickly under him and even the fighting dogs didn't charge their cages when he walked by. Thankfully, the kennel manager had taken pity on him when he arrived in the baron's household as a young boy alone in the world and so had let him sleep among the puppies and talk to the dogs as if they were friends. When Percy's favorite pup had been kicked by a horse and died wheezing and frightened in Percy's arms, the kennel manager covered Percy with a blanket and sat beside him all night, then walked into the forest with him and dug a hole for the pup, though pet graves were unheard of. When they returned to their work, there was something guarded and older about Percy.

When the Great Mortality arrived at the manor and all were fleeing, the kennel manager died outside the cages and the Master of Hounds held Percy back from running to him, then opened all the dog kennels before he fled. Everyone should fend for themselves, it was declared, so Percy headed for the coast, though he hadn't been home in a decade. Perhaps his mother was alive, though with every circling group of carrion crows he doubted it could be true. After a day's walk from the manor, Percy saw a wagon speed by with two dead children in the back, the farmer slumped over the seat and the horse frantic. By that evening, the only people Percy saw alive were a group of men flagellating themselves with barbed whips. At a crossroads, a massive man driving a corpse wagon, his eyes glazed over and his big shoulders drooping, stared hard at Percy. He lifted a hand to wordlessly point to the hamlet at the left fork and shook his head, like the gesture of Death itself. Percy chose the fork to the right.

The six dogs Percy worked with most often followed him. Two were hunting dogs who bounded into the forest along the way and dropped quail or rabbit at Percy's feet. He hung the bounty off his belt and called them back: he had no way to carry more than they could eat. Two were ratters that Percy had turned loose in the larder for rats that even the cats wouldn't hunt or would take to the rabbit warren when it was time to chase the does out of their holes for harvest. After several miles though, they trotted close to his heels unaccustomed to living outside their cages. Two dogs were broad-chested, steely-eyed fighters who were brought in at the end of a stag hunt to bring down the injured animal and Percy tied them together by their collars hoping that they were too stupid to coordinate their movements and so less likely to cause trouble.

The company of the dogs was a comfort to him and in addition to hunting his dinner, he relied on the dogs to keep him from horror. At the first hamlet, the hunting dogs sniffed the air and smelled death inside a building, so they turned tail and ran back to him, standing behind his leg. One morning Percy heard bleating, the dogs ran forward, and after calling out to people for permission to enter the farm, Percy found a large herd of frantic sheep trapped in a barn. He slid open the doors and they dashed into the paddock, leaving several lambs and an old ewe dead in the back of the building. Percy sighed, thinking of their fear as they realized that they were trapped, as their food ran out and their offspring died. In the paddock though, Percy could tell that they would graze the area to the ground, and he couldn't see a natural water source. They were still trapped. Commanding his dogs to stay by the edge of the barn, he walked through the herd. "Fences are for people," he told them quietly as if they were dogs, and he wedged open the gate at the far end of the field. If only they were his, he thought, as he strapped open the door to the barn to give them both shelter and freedom. If only they were his.

For years, Percy had been harboring a quiet desire to work the land. When the other dog tenders clustered in their quarters to drink ale and play cards, Percy sat in the grass behind the manor on the hill overlooking the farm and studied the farm family's decisions. What did they plant in the shade? Which plants needed full sun? Climbing plants were different from creeping plants. How were the chickens protected against the fox or the heat? Why did the girls crush eggshells to mix with the soil? What could be fed to the pig and what not? What did the vines look like when the harvest was inadequate? He watched their endless fight against blight and mold, snails, weasels, belly gas and hoof rot. And he smiled when he saw how contented the farmer seemed when she quietly tore beans off a bountiful pole for dinner.

But he was a dog-boy, nothing more. Recruited when he was eight years old, housed with others, fed from the kitchens at a communal table. He grew nothing, had no way to feed himself. And now that so many had died, what gentry survived who had dogs that needed tending?

On his journey, Percy made it his task to free any livestock trapped in barns or corrals. Many were dead but open gates, broken fences, and empty paddocks pleased him as evidence of animals free to forage.

Along the way, he fashioned saddle bags for the fighting dogs and filled them with the contents of smoke houses and good tools he found. But what use were the tools to him? He didn't have land on which to use them. He gathered them, nonetheless.

When he arrived at his home village, Wells-Next-the-Sea, he was comforted by the smell of the ocean but anxious over the silence that greeted his hellos. He hurried to his mother's cottage and called out to her, then stood pressed up against the wall beside the door, unable to enter. He looked at his dogs who showed no signs that there was carnage inside, but he still couldn't enter, and he finally slid down the outside wall to sit on his haunches. The dogs lined up against the cottage wall beside him and the ratters, who were not usually affectionate, climbed into his lap.

The village looked better than he remembered: the apple tree in front of his house was sturdy and heavy with unpicked fruit. Wildflowers were tall in the meadow just beyond the hamlet where wagons and horses usually trampled it bare. The whole place looked gentle now, and he remembered being happy and free to explore the beach with his mother always in sight. Running in the surf, bringing her prizes of stones and shells, so proud of himself, so full of love for her.

That had been his childhood, but not his mother's life. The hamlet had been built on the salt trade and his mother had spent her life in the surf, sluicing salt water into shallow pans that she set in the sun, then dumped and raked the salt that was left into small conical mounds. Her own mother, Percy's grandmother, bent and grizzled with scars, was finally too tired and old to beat the deep, fast-moving tide that swallowed the beach every day. She fell farther and farther behind as the salt gatherers retreated, and the villagers had to hold his mother and his aunt back until all they could do was watch their mother be swallowed by a wave.

Percy's mother's dress had a salt ring around the hem that finally rotted the fabric, and her feet and ankles had been spotted with open sores. The middle of the hamlet now held the broken-down remains of the firepits and cradles where pans were boiled, and Percy remembered that his aunt had had burns on her arms and hands from scooping the salt into bags. It was a forlorn little hamlet of drudgery where storms tore at the cottages and babies were born sickly and small. He had hated to leave her, but his mother was both elated and tearful when the baron's man came to recruit him: she had found a way to get him out.

Percy opened the cottage door with his back still against the wall and sent one of the hunting dogs in. When the dog came back to him with a placid expression, he stepped inside but slid down the wall and wept. So squalid, so rickety and windswept when he had been living with food every day in servants' quarters that seemed palatial in comparison. Tacked to the wall were the hand-colored labels and wrappings from the cheeses and nuts that he had sent home: a small gift from him, a luxury to be displayed by her. How much more could he have sent, he chided himself. How could he have left her here, in all this? When he collected himself, he retrieved from the mantle her small wooden comb, a single piece of lace too small for decoration, and a carved dog that he had made her just before he had been taken to the baron's kennels.

He dragged his heels, hung his head, and visited the hamlet's graveyard to see if there was a marker bearing her name, but he gave up the search when he found a single mass grave marked Citizens of Wells, 1350. The ships must have brought the plague to her before it had reached the manor. Her death was a tragedy, but her burial was a blessing, he decided, as he and his dogs returned to the cottage, ate from their packs and all curled up together on the floor. Percy wept long into the night, petting the dogs for comfort, and headed west again three days later, without a destination.

MT only knew one fact about her past: she had been taken to the nunnery when she was six. She had been transferred so many times, though, that she couldn't remember where she had been born, though it was one of the only questions ever asked of her. This much she knew: she had come from a graveled lane where her mother, thin with hunger, pushed her forward toward the nunnery doors. They'll feed you there, her mother had said, so MT's pursuit of food was relentless, as if feeding herself was the last request of her mother and that to obey it was to love.

In the nunnery, she ate bones from the scrap bucket, ate fat and gristle off plates that returned to the kitchen. She pretended to chase rabbits out of the garden but pulled up early carrots herself, brushing the telltale soil from her chin. Each time she opened her mouth to chew it was obeisance as well as penance for not taking a last look at her mother, for not remembering or inquiring where her mother was, for not seeking her out when the order fell apart during the Great Mortality and MT was free to roam; and especially it was penance for relentlessly punishing her mother in her heart for her abandonment, and since the woman's whereabouts were unknown, for not nursing her mother or even bearing witness to what had probably been the old woman's death. That meant that MT had abandoned her mother scores of times more than her mother's initial release.

Sometimes she thought that all the hours on her knees in devotion to the Holy Mother were actually prayers to her own mother, begging forgiveness, acknowledging her unworthiness. At one point she even resented the Holy Mother whose statues showed her well fed and clad in something other than rags like her own mother wore. In the market, when a father took a child into his arms and kissed its forehead, she felt privy to something obscene and turned away; when a mother nursed a baby, MT felt cut to the core. She had no language for that type of devotion, no intuitive connection to it; the sanctity of the family was a concept only, a rule without emotion.

The detachment gave her special courage during the plague years, though: the vision of the holy mother holding the broken son was reversed in her case. She grew up with a strange sense that her mother was the broken one in her arms and that she, by the grand design that had only two places in it, was the lamenting but healthy survivor. Her mother's sacrifice had been the tragedy in MT's life and somehow it meant that her debt was paid, and she could walk unscathed through the years of pestilence. Christ's sacrifice had ensured her soul and her mother's sacrifice had ensured her body.

So, she ate. She kneeled and prayed and when she was ten years old, the other nuns sniggered behind their hands at her odd shape and daily pushed her into the dirt in the garden. The Mother Superior brought her indoors to polish the woodwork and tend to the sage censer, which MT thought was a kindness, until she realized that the old woman did it to keep her out of sight. She grew wide but not tall and could polish and repair baseboards and wainscoting without kneeling. Lindenwood for statuary as well as reliable oak and temperamental walnut. The best bee's wax and oils to repair sun damage on the panels across from the windows; vinegar to kill mold on windowsills that leaked; a yearly scraping with a small trowel for carvings encrusted with soot. As for the sage, it grew low to the ground and harvesting it meant that she was an easy target for the bootheels of the other nuns, so she harvested at night and if caught out of her cell by the Mother Superior, the old woman returned her to her room without comment nor kindness.

Feeding and being fed. Her life had been built around it.

Despite the horror of the plague though, it had delivered her from a life where she had to scrounge for food to a life where food seemed to be everywhere. She woke up one morning peering at a long line of white stones circling a hedge, but they were eggs from feral chickens. She gorged herself until the yellow yokes caked the front of her habit. During a wind storm the fruit flew off the laden trees like cannon balls and she had to take shelter under the cart.

There had been food everywhere, except here in this manor house. Striding down the hallway of the manor toward the kitchen as the *faux* baroness, MT noted the rat droppings in the corners and the dust that caked the ledges, the cracked paneling where robbers had forced their way through windows. There was wood in need of tending but the first task was to get her flock fed. *Not her flock*, she admonished herself. The baroness's new staff.

In the kitchen, women curtsied when she came in and it surprised her then embarrassed her. Still, progress was being made. The room was getting warm, the steamy aroma of rabbit stew was curling into the air, and she couldn't help but snatch a carrot from the counter and relish its crunch. The kitchen maids were surprised, and MT made a mental note: apparently royals don't eat vegetables right from the garden. *Their loss*, she thought. She breathed deeply, nodding her appreciation and touching each woman on the forearm, which surprised them again.

But just as MT was filled with hope, she suddenly darkened with fear. What if the sheriff or the wagon drivers who had been denied their profits returned? The location for the new jail was clearly a short ride away, which made them vulnerable to a nighttime raid and could jeopardize their escape as well. *We must protect my manor*, she thought, then corrected herself. *She was protecting the women, that's all*. She abandoned her carrot and summoned the tall orphan lad who hurried with her to the front gate. Safety was paramount. Even if it was just for the night. Or the week. They closed the front gate and barred it, then walked quickly through the orchard and kitchen gardens to the back gate, which hung askance on rusted hinges.

"No, this will not do," she said nervously. "Go to the... stables and bring hammer and nails. Pegs if there are no nails. Seal it shut until we can improve the latches and locks. We'll not be besieged. When you're finished, station yourself and the old man on the top of the porter's lodge with a bell to sound the alarm."

"The alarm for what, milady?"

"The sheriff... or anyone who approaches."

The child ran off and MT quickly paced the perimeter of the yard checking the integrity of the garden walls, then back into the house to inspect the buttery, the storerooms, stables and pantries, then windows in every room in half of the house. No need for the other half if they're only staying for a bit. She and several maids sealed the other wing off with a sideboard in front of the door. In the morning, they would check that no trees or shrubs grew close enough to the garden wall to be climbed. These were desperate times, and these men had already kidnapped peasants once. There was no reason to think that they wouldn't try it again.

MT heard hammering at the back gate and went into the library, gingerly touching the poultice that clung to her chin. She usually went out of her way to avoid her reflection, but today she tentatively stepped to the mirror on the closet door. The black cap with its glass shards made her chuckle. Lightening bursting through the black, she thought, shredding a nun's habit. The rebellion of joy against misery. Her ideas, her command, finally seeing the light. That she could assume the confidence and poise of this woman, this baroness, was as much a charade as the clothing, she thought. And this dress! Imagine having the wealth and power to force a seamstress to not just cobble something together to cover her but to have it tailored to her shape. She climbed the stairs to the desk and while she thought of the bag of gold hidden near her feet, she opened the ledger on the desktop. Fine leather. Flawless paper.

Claudia, with the baby strapped to her in a sling, knocked and entered. She locked the door behind her.

"You should...study your lineage...milady. Have you found a Bible or book of heraldry?"

"Here's the chart of accounts. But you're right. Uncles. Cousins. Contenders. At some point we need to know who may be arriving to challenge us."

"Please find it." Claudia sounded almost panicked. She surveyed the empty bookshelves with her hands on her hips. "What we need is a diary or list of events."

MT opened every drawer in the desk. She went to the open closet and lifted a hatch where she had found the tall socks. Nothing. She opened the adjacent hatch and rummaged through the nightgowns and underclothes. "Here. The family Bible."

Claudia snatched it from her hand and opened it to the front pages, where the family tree was inscribed. She couldn't read, but she knew her numbers and there should be a date of birth. She ran her finger down the list, stopped, and sighed deeply.

"No record of her," Claudia said under her breath.

"No record of whom?" MT said and when Claudia turned away, MT followed her. "Of whom, Claudia?"

She pulled the baby closer.

"You have *my* secret," MT said, *though not all of them*.

Claudia took a deep breath and whispered. "She is the little lady of the manor, child of the baroness. She's the inheritor of the estate. More valuable if she was a boy, of course."

MT went slack jawed with shock. "You have kidnapped the child of a royal?"

"Not exactly. Besides, there's no evidence of her birth. You don't see a name, do you? They didn't even bother to record it! She is…cast off."

MT threw up her hands. "A mother would scour the earth to find her daughter!"

Claudia was defiant. "They died. Both of them."

"How do you know?"

"Because I was there," Claudia said.

MT was glad that real royals would not be arriving, but the relief was temporary. "What if a distant relative shows up to claim the land? Without the baby all of this belongs to the king."

"No, without *you*, all belongs to the king. We're no worse off than we were."

"Other than being strung up for kidnapping, crimes against the crown, fraud!" *And theft*, MT thought.

"I won't give her up. I won't." Claudia strode across the floor, holding the baby's head against her shoulder, resolute and powerful. "Make your intentions clear… 'milady!' Will you try to take her from me? Declare your position now or I'll leave tonight."

"No, no. Don't get your back up. I don't want her," though MT corrected what seemed harsh. "Not that she's unworthy, but that I am. I don't know anything about children. And just because I look like the baroness, I'm no more her mother than you are."

"If caught, I suppose we could say we were hiding her…

for her protection." Claudia knew the argument was weak.

MT paced the floor. "This will not work! We wouldn't be so lucky as to have her grow enormous and blonde like you. What happens if she is short…like me? Like her mother. Was the baron tall? Or at least of normal height? What color is her mother's hair?"

"No one knows. She always wore that damnable cap!" Everyone, guests, servants, tenants turned away from her when they saw their own reflection distorted in the mirrors. "I don't intend to be here as she grows! And even if I did, she's made of my milk: I am more her mother than anyone alive!"

"Who are you," MT demanded. "Who are you really?"

Claudia had been the family's wet nurse. With the lord and lady's child in her arms at all times, the baby blanket embroidered with gold and fringed with fur, she had walked through the servants' quarters and kitchens with an air of authority, but when she walked into the family's rooms she became invisible. An unnoticed but sharp observer of human interactions. She would have been the unseen carrier of a prize if the baby had been male, but as the child was a girl, both of them were nothing. She could have been a mule in a dress for all the gentry cared, as long as she and her clothing were clean, the breast milk didn't darken the front of her dress or dot the floor as she left the room. She had never met the bishop though he visited, and she had only seen the back of the sheriff as they spirited him into the library and closed the door.

The baroness was rarely concerned about the health or development of the child. The lady gave Claudia extra coins when she nursed the baby in the lady's chambers, which the baroness had her do to convince her ladies in waiting that she actually cared for the child. In fact, Claudia, who had been taken on just before the baby's birth, thought that the baroness had probably been horrified by it all. By the sex that made the baby, the obscene bulging of her body, the horror of its birth, the defeat of its gender, the disappointment of her husband, the tribulations of the baby's shit, piss and food. The baroness's milk dried up almost instantly, much to her relief. Claudia could only remember one instance when the lady had even held the child. Claudia had carried her into the baroness's sitting room and slid her into her mother's arms.

"She is thriving, milady," Claudia had said. "Let me show you how strong her legs are."

"Put her in the cradle," the lady said gruffly and handed her back. The swaddled baby lay there, untouched and unnoticed; she grew glassy eyed and incurious.

The lord had never held her, spoken to her, made any provisions for her at all. No announcement of her birth, no celebration. Apparently not even recorded. The only time the baron paid her any attention was when he insisted that Claudia nurse with her breasts exposed in his private sitting room.

"I shall kiss the little one," he said and bent over Claudia's bared breast to kiss the child's head, shaming Claudia with his arousal.

As no one else had any care for the child, Claudia intended to nurse her far longer than necessary and whenever they were alone, Claudia sang to her, taught her to clap, gave her things to explore with her mouth. But she had had to be careful: she took the baby outside to show her the budding trees and was immediately told to take the infant back to the nursery. Apparently the lady didn't want anyone to see her.

On the other hand, Claudia had sat sedately in the lady's chambers like the woman who could: could nurse when the lady wouldn't. Could give the child warmth and care while the lady was cold. The secret, though, was that she couldn't. Endless supplies of milk, but she couldn't give birth to a baby who could make it past a second Sunday. She gave birth to children who had been smaller than a loaf of bread. Failure had driven her to the manor. Her father died of the drink, then her mother's hens stopped laying and mold overtook their crops. Despite their best efforts, they had to start killing the livestock to survive, and her husband had run off to the city because she couldn't bear a living child, he had said, though Claudia knew it was as much because of his own inability to grow crops.

Her mother had walked out of the forest and returned several days later, then took Claudia – still grieving and healing from childbirth – and walked her to the baroness's manor to earn her living with her breasts. "You're a smart girl," her mother said as they walked. "I see you at the fairs and festivals: you understand people and the way the world works. You'll be fine." Her mother muttered little directives as they walked. Keep her opinions to herself. Scrub under her breasts every night and soften her nipples with butter. Every day thereafter, Claudia missed the trees, the smell of the soil and the lilacs, the new shoots and the first harvest, her mother, whom she assumed had now died in the Great Mortality, and the little babes who had been hers for mere moments.

As the baroness's wet nurse, she had tucked the extra coins the lady had given her into a little pouch that was held tightly underneath her breasts. Coins that were still safe, and now that the parents were dead maybe the little girl was safe too. After death had taken so many, maybe there was no one to take the baby away or tell her what to do.

The day the household had abandoned reason and fled without a destination began when little April, a serving girl who was barely more than a wisp of hair, crumbled onto the newly scrubbed floor of the hall, unable to breathe. The serving platter hit the stone floor with a clang and the spring peas and new carrots rolled onto the floor.

This was the first they had seen of the Great Mortality, though the stable boys and the Master of Arms had heard of a death that started in the lungs and was nearly instantaneous. It was sweeping north from London and the household had been nervously watching it creeping toward them in the east. That day, Claudia and others rushed to April, not yet hardened and selfish as the contagion would make them later. The house boy who carried April in his arms stumbled, wheezing, and fell before he could get her into bed. The old washerwoman who had taken a shine to April clutched her chest as she said her last prayers at the girl's side and the three died together.

The women of the house began shrieking, backing away from the bedroom, and anyone whose face was rosy from crying, or sweaty and ruddy from scrubbing the floor was suspected of being ill and others pressed themselves into the walls of the hall to step around them. Then it seemed as if death was coming at them from all directions as reports arrived of the death of the thresher, the stablemen, the farmers. Servants who had no permission to even enter the dining hall began running down the main corridor discarding their aprons and tools.

The sound carried to the sitting room of the lord of the house who had heard reports and dismissed them as problems of the city while quietly planning to escape in a carriage and two wagons to their northern manor. They all pulled away from the manor house as fast as the horses could be buckled in. If the baby had been a boy and the heir apparent, he would've ridden in the carriage with his parents but as she was not, she and Claudia were relegated to the very back of the first wagon.

They flew over the rutted roads, those in the carts holding on for dear life, certain the horses would stumble as they were whipped, their eyes as frightened as the lord and lady.

Just ten miles from home, there was a great banging on the roof of the carriage, the tired horses were pulled up short which made the first wagon nearly slam into the carriage. The carriage door opened, and the baroness tumbled out, crawled on the ground like a crab, grinding her dress into the dirt, then clung to the grass on the side of the road as her chest heaved with the struggle to breathe and she fell on her face, dead.

The baroness's chief lady-in-waiting ran to the Lady's side, wailing over the woman who, without her imperious manner and aggressive tone was now just an unnaturally short, round bundle of satin and fur. The baron, in an unusual show of empathy for his wife, came to her side and then fell in the grass beside her, followed by the Sargent at Arms who stumbled and fell unceremoniously at their feet.

The driver drove the empty carriage away at breakneck speed and then all hell broke loose. The servants in the last wagon leapt down and ran in all directions into the forest; the Men at Arms who were responsible for protecting the cases of silver plate and gold candlesticks that had been ready packed, abandoned their posts and their prizes to the highwayman, though Claudia was sure she saw at least one pull a package from the stack and run off with it. The ladies-in-waiting sat frozen in fear, with good reason, Claudia thought, as they lacked the skills to live wild in the forest and they couldn't bring themselves to rush to the Lady's side. The primary Lady-in-Waiting was now sitting on the ground like a peasant girl, grabbing at the collar of her dress and flushing with the first signs of sickness.

Claudia's only thought was to protect the baby, and she hurried down from the wagon, throwing the edge of the gold embroidered and fur-trimmed blanket over the little one's face. With the baby in one arm and her hiked-up dress in the other hand, she ran northeastward down the road.

But a woman of her size can't run for long despite her strong, healthy legs and lungs and as she slowed the blessed silence of the countryside overtook her. There was no one running behind her, no sign of servants or men at arms, just Claudia and the precious baby who began fussing for a meal.

Claudia stepped off the road into the forest, found a log to sit on and the baby latched on to begin that sweetest of communions. "Poor little orphan," Claudia cooed to her, still breathless from the run and the fear. "Though you are perhaps better off without such a cruel and dismissive mother," she said though she regretted her lack of generosity for a woman who had just passed. "What's to become of you now?" No parents, no home. A little penniless lady, with a title but no more resources than her own child would have had.

After the baby had had her fill they set out again, though she kept to a deer trail parallel to the road. It wouldn't do to encounter other people, partly for fear of contagion, for fear that the gold embroidery would attract thieves, or that the baby would be shuttled off to the queen's court. After the next feeding, Claudia rested her feet and decided to rid the blanket of the gold embroidery. She set the baby in a patch of soft moss and a ray of sunshine to kick her feet and explore her hands while Claudia picked the satin layer of the blanket away from the batten inside. She tore her own slip into several new diapers and as they wandered through the forest, she washed the dirty diapers in the creek, rung them out, and hung them on her belt to dry. Now the little one was an ordinary child in the arms of an ordinary woman. Claudia decided to call her Daisy.

The forest was kind to them. A cow she encountered in a forest clearing, lowing with pain over its engorged udder, was grateful when she milked it straight into her mouth. Claudia took off its bell, as it seemed that there was no one in the world to herd it and the wolves didn't need notification.

She had never lived in a world so quiet, so devoid of wagon wheel and hammer.

In their wanderings, Claudia came across a toddler crying at the corpse of her mother and Claudia desperately wanted to cross the road and soothe the child until her older sister, no more than eight years old, stepped from the woods and with a steely glance at Claudia, grabbed her sister by the hand and the two ran away. Claudia wondered what she would have done for the children if they had stayed, if she would have risked contagion, risked Daisy to help them. After that first encounter, she turned away from children if she saw them in the hedges, but at night it made her feel small and mean spirited. So many lost children and her lost without one.

Still, with Daisy on her chest, hidden in the shrubbery, she slept deeply and sometimes would stand up in the night, astounded by the stars and the contented, breathing forest.

When the season changed, they settled into a small hunting cabin deep in the woods.

Daisy grew robust, kicking and laughing, rosy-cheeked and fat. Claudia pressed berries into her lips to redden them which made Claudia laugh, and she raised the baby high in the air and kissed her cheeks. Daisy's eyes started to sparkle.

This was everything she had always wanted: a fat and happy baby, growing up surrounded by her love. A baby pawing at her, hungry for her, exploring her collar and sucking on her fingers, looking at her as if she was the whole world. A place for her care, a connection to the future, a companion like no other. Her life's ambition: to be a mother.

And yet Claudia blamed herself for their capture.

She was foraging in the forest with Daisy, the baby's sling stuffed with greens for soup, when the aroma of baked bread wafted toward Claudia.

She knew she should have kept her distance, as people meant disease, but the smell pulled her forward until she stepped out of the forest onto a small road that ran perpendicular to the one by her cottage.

An itinerant baker named Merek had stopped at the side of the road, his beehive-shaped clay oven on a handcart baking a tiny loaf which was the last scrap of dough he had, and it sent up its enticing smell.

A thin but muscular man, Merek had lost one of his hands as a child, and he stood with his right hand holding the stub of his left. He was so startled by another person that he whirled around and nearly fell, then grabbed the long baking peel he had attached to his cart and brandished it in her direction.

"Stay back," he barked.

"Easy now, baker," Claudia said. "I'm happy to keep my distance. The cozy ones die off in these times. It's just that your bread is such a welcome aroma."

"That's the last of it," he said sadly, lowering the peel. "I can gather berries and herbs all day but without someone to harvest the wheat and the bishop's mill to grind it, I am a man without a purpose." He knew there were other reasons, but he had grown accustomed to the half-truth. "Besides, there is no one left to eat it."

"May they rest in peace," she said.

He nodded as he lowered himself to the roadside, using his peel for support. "Please join me. From afar. Happy to share the last loaf."

Claudia sat on the other side of the road, bringing out the baby that she had hidden under her smock.

The baker lit up. "Well, there's a welcome sight! What's the tike's name?"

"Daisy," she said, hoping it sounded like a name well-used. "I'm Claudia."

"Merek."

The two silently inhaled the scent of the bread, more pungent it seemed because it was the last. No sense asking whether family had been lost or even what village they had come from, since the stories would break their shaky courage, and the village was probably abandoned now anyway. The bread came out of the oven and Merek, bouncing the hot loaf on one hand, carried it to a flat rock to the middle of the road and tore off half before retreating to his side.

Claudia retrieved it and bit into the crunchy and soft bread savoring the flavor, brought the bread close to Daisy's nose so she could inhale the beautiful aroma.

It may have been that the two strangers were so focused on the sad pleasure of the last bit of bread that, despite their sitting nearly in the road, they didn't hear the horses with a creaking wagon. Maybe it was because they both assumed it was still the days before the plague when a farmer transported parsnips or firewood, but it seemed that the sheriff was upon them in no time. Claudia hid the baby and she and the baker struggled to swallow the last bit of bread before the sheriff seized Claudia by the arms.

"Serfs are indentured to the land, which is where you're returning," Baudwin gruffly informed her.

"I'm no serf, sir," she said indignantly, but elaborated cautiously. If she told him she was the wet nurse to the baroness, the baby's identity would be known. "I'm a… member of the staff of the baroness." She struggled against his grip.

"Then you're in luck, because that's where you're going."

A guard grabbed the baker and heaved him to standing, then released him and jumped back when he saw the stump of his arm. The guard shoved the baker to the ground before turning back to the rest.

As the wagon lumbered forward, Claudia began to recognize the landmarks but everywhere she looked it was deserted. All the hamlets and crossroad inns. The chapels. Stable doors were open, paddocks empty, the shutters on the cottages open to the rain. When she arrived back at the manor that she had fled, she was in no position to mention that she had seen with her own eyes the baroness's body by the road. If they realized that the baron was dead, she might be carted off to another estate. Minutes after being shoved into the corral and guards posted at the door, however, Claudia had seen a woman remarkably like the baroness stride into the barn.

CHAPTER FOUR

Baudwin Pierce the sheriff was new to his job, unaccustomed to his unchecked power and while Claudia was being strong-armed from the road into the wagon, he had turned in his saddle to see that the baker had not been injured.

He had been forced into the job just last month by the earl who had seen him breaking up a fight in an ale house where the earl had stopped momentarily to drink a pint while holding a handkerchief over his nose. The earl snapped his fingers and motioned for Baudwin to come to him and muffled by the embroidered cloth, noted Baudwin's size, what the earl called his commanding presence, and without asking if Baudwin was interested in the job, the earl outlined a plan that was long on a description of elevated status, but short on actual details. Baudwin vaguely registered something about securing workers for the earl's estate, but he heard clearly the monthly stipend that would be given to him.

He was provided with a horse and a doublet bearing a

sheriff's insignia but soon was flanked by men whom the earl said were Baudwin's posse, his staff, and he had no choice but to quickly assume command. The first group of men they encountered came along willingly when Baudwin described the opportunity, and it seemed only reasonable that they should ride in a wagon. When women were forced into the wagons, Baudwin reasoned that women were needed on the estate as well and that they should ride separately so as to not be mistreated by strangers.

But soon Baudwin felt caught up in a whirlwind: transformed into a sheriff by muffled words through a handkerchief, turned into a leader of men when suddenly flanked by others; sent to do the bidding of the earl to first invite and then, he discovered, to kidnap peasants. By the time he understood the full extent of the plan and his place in it, he realized that the posse was staffed by so many large and brutal men that his protest would have endangered him and destroyed the only authority he had ever known. The bishop's involvement with the women stopped him from fully understanding their destination and when he erroneously heard that the scheme with its permanent jail and fortified barn had been the brainchild of the baroness, he arrived at the manor filled with anger that made him grind his teeth. He mistook MT's rage over the arrangement as the baroness's cruelty the posse had spoken of though never experienced. When he looked down on the top of the baroness's cap, ready to do verbal battle, the mirrors showed him a deep, terrifying pit.

He had to acknowledge that employment had been hard to come by. Years ago, he and his father had both been pressed into service in the king's army but on a day when his father found him barely alive on the battlefield, they bundled themselves up and sneaked away just before sunrise to live as woodcutters in the forest. It explained both his strength and his scars. The recent sickness had taken his father and with no brewery operating and half the population gone, there was little call for wood. Villages all around had been abandoned for lack of inhabitants and the survivors who clustered together could last for more than one winter on the woodpiles of their dead neighbors.

Now, as sheriff, surrounded by people who were profiting from cruelty but offering him more money than he had ever seen if he organized it, Baudwin embraced his authority as good fortune long overdue, and the task at hand was a laudable enforcement of the king's rule. If they wanted a jail, they would get a jail.

The plan, in fact, had been the brainchild of the earl. The earl's serfs on his southeastern properties had died in large numbers and last year when it had been confirmed that the baron's entourage had not reached York, that the baron's manor house had been ransacked and was now deserted, the earl knew he had to do something drastic. His power was waning, his cows un-milked and crops left neither planted nor threshed. It was an upending of his world more drastic than the plague, as he was rich in land but now, without anyone to work it, his coffers were emptying, and an earldom would be worth nothing since land that can't generate revenue is just dirt. The deserted barony would make a reasonable jail for the reluctant but the news that Baudwin the sheriff brought the earl when he reported back was a problem.

"Only the baroness has returned?" the earl asked, turning to the sheriff.

"Yes, milord."

"And where has this Medusa been since the baron's demise?

"Sequestered and grieving in the north, milord, though I dared not ask for details."

"Quite right," the earl said, mulling over his circumstance as he paced the room. Now he would have to deal with the baroness, a shrew whose voice was Satan's horn. He spun on his heel and looked back at the sheriff. Well, what of it? He was the earl, God damn it, and the barony was given by his largesse (though he knew it was really from the king). He could simply explain that building the jail and securing laborers was an arrangement between him and the baron. Who was she to question her husband? On the other hand, he had no desire to go to her to explain the situation and certainly didn't want to invite her to his abode.

"How did she seem when they arrived?"

"Incensed, milord." Baudwin said. "She insisted on keeping all the women."

"The young ones…the bishop's?"

"Indeed, milord. To reestablish her household, she said. I have the men…readied to build the jail, however."

The earl grunted and looked away. "I suppose a woman needs servants. Take the next batch of women to the bishop by way of a different route. They're his problem, not mine. Bring me men. Strong men to work the fields. Any men at all, for that matter."

~ * ~ * ~ * ~

Unknown to either the earl or the sheriff, several of the men who had been tasked with taking the young women to the bishop's brothels had circled back to the manor. They waited on horseback behind a stand of trees on the road, and as dusk fell, they charged up to the gate and dismounted. Surprised to see it locked, they pounded on it until the young boy and the old man peered over the parapet on the porter's lodge.

"Send out your redheads," one said, and his companion chuckled. "We're not greedy, just the redheads."

The old man ordered the orphan boy to find the baroness. The men outside shuffled and joked, tried to egg the old man on. They threw stones at the wall and flung their shoulders against the gate.

Finally, MT climbed to the parapet with a torch.

"You threaten the household of the baron?' she said in the deepest, most booming voice she could muster.

They heard her voice, but the torch and cap made her head a demon shooting flames. Their horses bolted back down the hill.

"The sheriff will hear of this," she continued, "and rest assured, the only red heads will be yours when I have you hung!"

The two men jostled each other, stunned by the demon head, muttering about the horses and the sheriff. They told themselves weakly that it wasn't worth the effort, as they backed down the hill and called unsuccessfully for their horses.

"Is the back garden door sealed?" she asked the orphan boy and when he nodded, she drew him close to sooth his fear. "Tomorrow you climb the trees to check the walls and windows."

In the manor library, MT made a pronouncement.

"No woman goes out of the wall unaccompanied. Have we captured any chickens?"

"Four of them; one is now laying," Claudia said.

"Then the children are to stay inside the wall as well. No foraging without an adult."

"I'm glad you were fierce with them. It buys us a little more time," Claudia said. "No one here knows you, but at some point word will get out and she was notoriously cruel."

MT waved the comment away. "Witnessing this much death will soften any heart."

"That reasoning might work," Claudia said and paced the floor, patting little Daisy in her sling. She walked up to MT, daring herself to look at the embroidered cap. Previously, she had looked away as she offered the child to the baroness because the cap had reflected nothing but gray fear. Today, with chubby and vibrant Daisy in her arms, it was a circus of baby hands and little bows.

"Should I be grieving for my husband *and* my child?" MT was perplexed.

"She took no interest in her," Claudia said.

"What would drive a family to completely ignore a newborn?"

"The fact that she's a girl."

"No. It has to be more than that. Royals may not celebrate their girls, but they use them as pawns in marriage. To not even record the birth, though! They denied her existence, really. Why would they do that?"

"I told you," Claudia said, "the baroness was cruel."

They looked at each other, both with doubt in their eyes.

There was a knock on the door of the library and both women jumped. Claudia mimed to MT: stand up straight and assume the rigidity of a baroness. MT pointed to Claudia: the discussion would be continued.

"You may unlock it," she ordered Claudia, who looked askance at being ordered. MT threw up her hands. Her new friend couldn't have it both ways, she smiled. "And bring me the key."

Claudia waved Gertrude into the room.

"Where will milady take dinner this evening?"

"How many bowls have we?" MT asked without looking up from the ledger on the desk, though she knew.

"Just five, milady. Four ladles but just two spoons. And two mugs."

"And where have we fires laid?"

"Naught but in the kitchen." Gertrude looked disapprovingly at Claudia who should have ordered it done in other rooms.

"Milady," Gertrude continued, "you understand that with

no hunter there will be no quail or boar. No duck, either. And without a mill we have no flour so no pies or biscuits. Besides, we have no tureen, no serving dishes. Not even chairs, milady!"

MT looked up. "We'll stand and eat out of buckets if necessary," she said. The cook didn't move. Claudia glared at MT over Gertrude, knowing the 'new baroness' would be tempted to eat in the kitchen with the others.

"Alright, make the stew a soup that can be drunk, set the bowls and tankards at places nearest me at the high table in the Great Room, the fruit and egg at the far end and while the first have soup, the others will have their fruit and egg. Then the bowls, tankards and fruit will change places, moving down the line. Tonight, we eat together."

"It's not fitting to have servants at the high table, even if standing!" Gertrude protested.

MT stared at the cook. "As it is the only table left…what would you suggest? We all stand around your chopping block?"

Gertrude scowled but curtsied.

"Lay a fire in the central hearth," MT ordered, as she touched the poultice that adhered to her wounded chin. "Just tonight, we eat together, as we are now all delivered."

Claudia shook her head with disapproval, then stiffened as Gertrude turned to leave. They would be lucky to convince anyone of MT's royal stature even to the end of one day with the mistakes this woman was making, but Claudia was too tired to venture back onto the road, especially with the sheriff rounding people up and the narrow miss just now. It's a good thing Daisy is still on the breast, she thought patting the baby again. Good to be inside an actual house, warmed by a hearth, and given a chance to rest. Now it was in her best interest to help this little potato-faced woman who looked so like the baroness it was uncanny.

~ * ~ * ~ * ~

MT spent the rest of the day striding from pantry to post in her new domain. After a year of digging graves amid horror, then three quarters of a year alone on the road with her bearskin pelt and her cart, she was almost giddy to be behind solid walls, surrounded by women again. Eggs that had been found in the shrubbery or just laid were treated like pearls; spoons and dented bowls, including hers, were celebrated.

She could manage this, couldn't she? Even if just for the time it took to get rid of the sheriff and slip away.

She had seen transformations before. When she was eight years old, she had watched a jolly Mother Superior's skirts flying out in front of her as she strode the halls orchestrating change. To young MT, it was the best kind of dancing. "You, little one," the woman said, stopping abruptly in the hall and bending to take MT by the elbow. "Read everything you can find. Know numbers and money. Learn to write with a strong hand. Study maps. God has given you something special up here," she said and tapped MT on the temple. When MT was 12 and shuffled off to another nunnery, eight months of miserable malnutrition was brought to an end by the arrival of a new abbess who barked orders, disgusted by the state of things. MT followed at her elbow soaking up the lessons on efficiency, gardening, irrigation and animal husbandry. Food had never tasted so good. When she was 16, moved yet again, she huddled at night inventing plans with an errant nun who was frequently punished but still had a giddy ingenuity. They whispered their ideas and giggled behind their hands.

Today, she tried to finally put into action all that she had learned. "Take only the fruit on the ground for now," MT ordered. "We don't want to shock the trees in our hunger." She proceeded to the garden, today's white cap sparkling in the sunshine like a crown. "Leave the last of the carrots so they can make more. And save the tops, of course. We have more need of seedlings than pig feed." She was more directive than she had ever been and apparently knew about more than just wood and wax! Every peasant had a kitchen garden but some of these women had been maids, and in the house of the gentry apparently no one did anything without direct orders. They stood trance-like in front of her, and she wasn't sure if they were looking at her face or the cap. Sometimes, they crossed themselves, as if seeing a martyr. "The fennel stalks will make good bedding," she said decisively. "Shake the seeds into a cloth and carry the stalks inside. No, call that child back. We'll ignore the dovecote today. No sense gathering fertilizer until we have the gardens tilled. An extra egg for anyone who can lure a cat," she proclaimed.

That afternoon, Jacob the warrener arrived with a crate of rabbit already dressed for the stewpot and MT smiled broadly as he approached. He seemed more joyful than anyone she had ever met.

"From Eleanor of Aquitaine," he said, as he bowed to her, but didn't explain the names of the pillow mounds or the expanse of the land called the coneygarth.

What a deliciously imaginative young man, she thought, *and so handsome*. She motioned for a girl to take the crate. "Please thank Queen Eleanor for me, and I appreciate your… delivery, Jacob." He lit up like she had given him rubies.

That night, she slid between the bearskin and the bedclothes and closed her eyes, enveloped by the musk and weight of the bearskin, her refuge. In the morning, she donned the white cap again, all awoke to mugs of steaming broth, though they had to share tankards, and they set to their tasks. "I want to show you my land," she told Claudia as they stood in front of the hearth, and Claudia noted the ease with which the little woman declared her possession of the property. "And survey the damage during my absence," MT continued.

They stopped in the kitchen. Gertrude the cook turned on them.

"There's no sense harvesting more than I can put up and I've nothing to put anything up with or in," she snapped. "Milady." She curtsied. MT spoke but Gertrude didn't hear her, feeling her ire drain away as she watched the gold thread embroidery and glass gems on the baroness's cap. It was the type of grandeur she longed to be around: the finery and glittering jewels of royalty. Perhaps the cap was a portent of her advancement; perhaps when the household was restored this baroness would surround herself with the opulence Gertrude had always wanted to see. She had no illusions that the grandeur would be hers, but just to be near it, to have her jellies and roasts consumed by important people in their finery. Head Cook of the baroness. Sounded grand. Then Gertrude remembered where she was: at this point it was all rabbit stew, rabbit broth. A few early carrots thrown in. Maybe she was destined to just be a drudge. She was more like the stag being torn apart in the cap's embroidery than the jewels surrounding the scene.

"Gertrude," MT said, to startle the cook out of her revery. "There is no sense in letting it all go to seed, either. We'll dry in the sun what we don't need immediately." She turned to Claudia. "Have someone look for drying racks or order them built."

Crossing the yard, MT's cap had a warm glow from the morning sun. Claudia tried to think of the last time this house was peopled by happy, relaxed women. A saint's day perhaps, or a time when the baroness had been away.

A girl ran to the pair. "Shall we harvest the fishpond, milady?"

MT stopped. Fishpond? She didn't know about a fishpond. "Show me. I haven't… seen it lately."

The weeds had grown up the wooden collar of the fishpond, algae obscured the surface, and the fish were thick inside.

"Yes, clear this out, and harvest a few. They'll be glad of the room. Take them to the cook to see if she wants them dried or eaten tonight."

As Claudia and MT crossed the front courtyard, the young lookout was instructed to climb down from the parapet and lock the gate behind them. They set out to first assess the size and health of the woodpile.

"Our goal is to bring everything we need within these walls," MT said. "Including the woodpile."

Claudia nodded. It was not only safer for the women, it would slow the spread of gossip about the baroness and the imposter if everyone was kept inside the walls.

MT pondered. "The largest unused space is the courtyard between the main gate and the door."

"The madam would never tolerate something so unsightly in the front."

"Perhaps the madam has changed in more than one way."

"No, you cannot vary that much," Claudia said under her breath, though there was no one nearby. "No woman of stature would tolerate it. Dead giveaway."

MT clucked. "Very well. What about the outbuilding nearest the front gate?"

"Bugs."

"Could we keep the chickens nearby?"

"I suppose we could rotate them between the garden and the woodpile." Claudia looked behind them. "You really have no idea what you're doing, do you?"

"No. I've seen it done but never done it. Any peasant is more equipped than I am."

"You're certainly good at giving orders, though," Claudia chided, and the women smiled.

At dinner around the high table in the Great Room, Claudia watched MT and even though she couldn't see her reflection in the cap, the embroidered scenery of a lion killing a stag was ferocious and gruesome, and the bandage on her chin sported a brown spot of old blood.

MT stood at the head of the table where a platform allowed her to stand with her head slightly higher than the others. *Shrewd woman*, MT thought, *this monster of a baroness, finding a way to keep power despite her size*. But it was the first time the women could look her in the eye, and she wondered if that would unmask her. It hardly mattered, though. They were standing, not sitting, at a table in a house just barely better than the barn they had been in. For her, it was hardly an improvement from the spot under her cart covered by bearskin. The fires were just beginning to take the chill off the air. No brooms had been fashioned to sweep the floor or battle the cobwebs in the corners. They were a band of frightened women dwarfed by an empty house.

"Mary, Mother of God," MT said, and all lowered their gaze. "We bless you for delivering us from the hands of evil." Several of the younger women started to tremble. "We rejoice in your generosity," she said, hoping it would divert the young women's mind from the past. "We take your beauty, grace and fortitude into our hearts… that have been softened now by our ordeal. May we honor you by good work, kindness to others and a deep understanding of the miracle of your bounty. With Ann at the head and Bridget at the foot, bless this house and all who dwell within her. Amen."

It was the first time since she had been a novice that she

had prayed with genuine thanksgiving and tonight it was with a true longing to protect others. With love for them, possibly. She tried on the emotion. Love. Perhaps she understood Claudia who had not set the baby down even once.

"Where is the old man?" she asked one of the maids as they passed the first tankard of soup to her.

"In the kitchen with the cook, milady."

"Ah. Near the fire. Will you all sleep there tonight?"

"Aye. As the pantries are bare we've laid down boughs. We'll lay a fire in your room, directly, milady."

MT nodded her agreement. "Claudia, you may accompany me."

"Very good, milady. I thank you."

After dinner MT and Claudia went into the library.

"You understand that we cannot stay here," Claudia said to her pointedly. "Putting up vegetables and drying fish? You're acting like you're making plans for winter. It's been a decent ruse while we feed ourselves and wait for the sheriff to move on, but this is not... permanent. We should be devising a way to flee."

"You're right," MT said with a sigh. "I had planned to just rescue the women, free the prisoners, get a bit to eat for all of us and then escape with the gold."

"Gold?!" Claudia moved Daisy to the other hip and glared at MT. "What gold?"

MT sighed deeply over her slip of the tongue.

"You need to tell me exactly what you have done!" Claudia demanded.

MT told Claudia of her life as Sister Mary Thomas, how she had stumbled drunkenly into this new identity. Claudia looked at her pointedly, waiting for the mention of gold. MT padded to the desk, kicked the lever, got off the elevated chair, and pulled the bag of gold from its hiding place. She omitted mention of the small quantity in her tattered habit.

Claudia went down on one knee and ran her hand through the coins, letting them drop from her fingers, awestruck.

"Think of all the good that can be done with this, Claudia," MT said as she dipped her own hands into the bag. "If it's used for a good purpose it isn't stealing, is it? We can consider it a donation. From the baroness. Don't you see, Claudia, now I can do something of real value?"

Claudia clambered off the floor and held Daisy tighter. She backed away from MT. "I…I cannot be involved in this." She was flustered, panicked. As much as she longed for a life with money, the punishment for theft was horrible. "They will…"

"I'll share it with you, of course!" MT quickly assured her. "As soon as we devise a way out of this."

Just as MT rose from the floor to plead with Claudia, the alarm bell bounced off the walls of the manor.

"More intruders?" MT asked, and quickly stuffed the bag back into its hiding place. She pulled on her boots and cape. "Tell the women to lock themselves in the pantry," she ordered, as she flung open the door and headed outside.

MT called up to the boy standing watch. "Who is it?"

"The sheriff, milady."

When MT arrived at the barn, a new set of prisoners was being stuffed into the corrals.

"No women this time?" she asked venomously as Baudwin stood with his arms crossed over his chest, his legs spread wide.

"We...thought better of that," he said, though MT wasn't convinced.

"Two of your men were here tonight making demands," she said as she scanned the posse for them.

"My men are all here, milady, and have been with me since we saw you last."

MT shook her head. Must have been the bishop's men. "And it is necessary that you seize these men rather than simply offer them employment?"

Baudwin didn't look in her direction. "Ordinance of Laborers. Serfs off the land are to be returned or imprisoned."

MT paced around the barn. At the last corral, she turned to pace back and consider what to do next when a man grabbed the hem of her dress.

"Well...if it isn't Empty the None," he said, and MT's breath caught in her throat.

CHAPTER FIVE

Empty the Nun: it was a name she hadn't heard in quite a while. It had been given to her by the roadside thief who had helped her dig graves. She had tenuously accepted his offer of help though she had kept her distance, staying in her cloud of sage smoke as much as she could, sitting on the opposite side of the fire from him at night, turning a blind eye to his pilfering in exchange for his doing half, then most, of the digging.

His name was Simon, a fletcher whose family made arrows that in the rare times of peace were used by royal hunting parties, but for all of Simon's life, for the army. The family rode amid the cooks and armorers to battlegrounds, crafting shafts from saplings, gluing the fletches to the arrows and attaching the lethal iron tips just after they were fashioned by the army's traveling blacksmith.

He had been born in the back of a wagon. His mother, usually placid as she attached fletches amid a veritable nest of duck wings, screamed like the far-off sounds of men who were just then dying on the battlefield, and she stained the wagon with blood and gore like the wagon that retrieved the dead. His father had rolled barrels of arrows at the perimeter of the wagon to extend his wife's privacy beyond the mounted tent and he barked at anyone nearby to give a wide berth, trying to burn off a fear of death that had suddenly come too close to home, a fear that even after a lifetime of war had never chilled his blood as this did.

The celebration of Simon's birth was frenzied, twisted, life amid death, announced to men whose blood was filled with rage, the little bundle of him held up in triumph as a warrior would the heart of his enemy. Drunk on ale, his father boasted of his son and the 800,000 arrows delivered to the king the previous year as if he had fashioned them all himself.

Throughout his childhood his mother had kept Simon close, teaching him to stir the pot of rabbit glue, then tie the fletches with string and pack the arrows together in barrels so tightly that they barely jostled, points down, fletches lightly fluttering in the breeze. He had sat on his mother's lap as she pointed out the birds, the types of trees, recited stories to him and rocked him. He was happy and calm, oblivious to the war around him. At ten years old, his father had assigned him to run bundles of arrows to the archers at the front lines, against his mother's wishes, and at 12, when his mother had run out of excuses and had become too weary to fight about it any longer, his father forced him to join the arrow boys. It was the day his childhood ended.

The young arrow boys (sons of the blacksmith, carpenter

and cook) were sent into the field after the battle to collect the arrows that had fallen far short onto empty ground. It was close enough to the war that soon Simon developed an apprehensive nature, a nervous sense of impending doom. The older the boys got, the closer to the carnage they were expected to go. Simon and the teenage boys, just before they were old enough to become soldiers, were given the grisly and dangerous assignment of moving into the second ring of battle, pulling the arrows from in and among the corpses. It was a job that first frightened the boys, then hardened them, and finally filled them with a cruel bravado that they took out on each other at night.

When Simon was 14, the other arrow boys challenged him to go beyond even the second ring and accompany the armorer's son into what had been the center of the battle, where arrows never flew, the scene of hand-to-hand combat where the corpses, despite their armor, weren't felled by a single, neat entry point, but hacked to death with swords, gutted with lances, trampled by horses into a whole new level of horror. The boys were expected to retrieve pikes from the bloodied ground, wrest lances from dead hands and extract swords from mangled torsos, pull the dagger from a lifeless gut, and wrestle a dead man from his armor, all tasks that seemed as violent as the battle itself. Knights' jewel-encrusted or silver inlaid swords were usually left at home for ceremonies, and their second-best weapons were kept with the retrieved bodies of the nobles or claimed as prizes by the opposing knights the minute the battle was over. Most of what the armorers gathered were plain, unadorned weapons, shields and breastplates that they threw into a cart to be cleaned of blood and flesh, resharpened, reused, retrieved again after the next battle. It made the armorer's son dead-eyed and the armorer cruel.

As a teen, Simon had taken the challenge to go into the very center of the battle only once and on his way back through the gruesome maze, shaking so hard that he was unsteady on his feet, he picked up an overlooked arrow. A wounded boy soldier whose doublet was torn to the waist grabbed Simon's leg and begged for help but Simon, whether crazed with the gore he had witnessed or enraged by the challenge from the other boys that had sent him there, plunged the arrow into the little soldier's left shoulder, pulled it out, turned it, and drove it in again until the soldier passed out with a star-shaped wound above his heart.

Simon walked away from his parents the day of the boy's impaling, throwing down the arrows, his apron and arm protectors that were dark with old blood and splattered red from that day. Without a word, he glared at his father, then rolled up his blanket. His mother sighed sadly but hurried to tie dried meat and the last of their cheese into a cloth for him. She pressed it to him but said nothing, as if a lifetime around carnage had rendered her mute for this last sadness or perhaps fearing that if she gave voice to this sorrow, the sluice gates would open to her outrage at the rest. She pushed him toward the open road, willing to live without him just to spare him the life his father lived. He never saw either of his parents again.

The one who stayed with him forever, though, was the

ghost of the impaled boy. That night and every night thereafter, including the one before his capture by the sheriff, Simon dreamed of the boy's hand clutching Simon's ankle; of the wound, the star, the sight of the arrow breaking through skin, the contorted face of the boy in pain. Sometimes Simon woke whimpering, sometimes clutching his shoulder, but always exhausted and sickly with guilt. He tried to banish the ghost with ale, to beg it for respite, bargain with it, threaten it, and more than once he had drawn wary glances at a roadside inn when others heard him pleading in his nightmares, or pounding his head against the wall. He longed for a quiet night of uninterrupted sleep. As close as he ever got to peaceful sleep were the nights when he dreamt of falling to his knees to ask the ghost for forgiveness, but when he opened his mouth no sound came out, no matter how hard he pushed. Sometimes in the dreams he clawed at his throat and pulled out shards of glass. Or he transformed into a dog, licking the ghost-boy's feet, then rose as a crow and pecked at the specter's eye sockets. He awoke either tortured and powerless or having committed further sins against the boy.

As a grown man, Simon saw the battles even when awake, like the one against the French when the sky was black with crows that he had to beat away with a staff before he could retrieve arrows. On bleak days, he remembered the especially brutal battle when the enemy (it could have been any of them) cut the men into pieces and left them in the sun. Or the war against the Scots where the cries of the wounded could be heard all the way back to camp and his mother went to bed with a cloth wrapped around her ears. How many times had his leg been grabbed by a man holding his own entrails, as if he, a little boy, could do anything against death?

When he met MT it seemed to Simon that the only survivors of the Great Mortality were scavengers. Crows, wolves, beetles and rats. This plague was another feast for the crows and the sound of their cawing made him twitch. More than once, he had stopped at the crossroads, unable to direct his horse or choose his path because he was crippled by the sound of his childhood – the cackle of birds in their ragged celebration of another corpse.

The remaining people he saw were scavengers as well: those who could scrounge and dig, make something of remnants and cast-offs, remake themselves with the property of others.

To Simon, happy people lived in a different world, and he felt miles away from them even when he sat in a crowded market. They danced across a river where the heat made their figures ripple and wave. In an unknown country, speaking a foreign tongue. So why dance around the May Pole or learn to play the lute, he wondered. Why marvel at the sunshine or the pointless flowers when all was soon to be putrid rot and sorrow? Why sing and stumble drunk around the fire when the harvest meant that someone would fall off the hay wagon and die in the morning. From the smallest bun to the newest bridge, everything had a flaw. It was as if he sat at a heaping banquet table searching for the gristle.

He kept to himself, dark and sullen. No point making friends when betrayal was sure to be the outcome. Men shied away from him in the alehouse when he dismissed their endeavors and didn't laugh at their jokes. They bought drinks for others and moved to far tables. Women in the markets could see his darkness from the way he shuffled, and they charged him extra, gave him castoffs, as if taxing him for the gloom he carried into their world. Even in the brothels, women considered him a chore, as he arrived without gifts or even hollow compliments and did his business without glee. He was a hunched-over man, so accustomed to bending over the dead to retrieve arrows or steal trinkets that he was crumpled over on himself, legs more like a frog than a man.

While he longed for absolution from the ghost boy, he didn't apologize to others: not for tripping someone with outstretched feet, splashing them when he dismounted or any of the little discourtesies and blunders of normal life, and not for the swindles he committed that left a child without food, or the lies that made up the bulk of his profit.

The world deserved his skillful larceny, he assumed. As a teenager first out on his own, Simon was a good thief because no one suspected him of such treachery and cunning. By the time he was a young man, he was so adept that he could make things disappear from the most unlikely places: the well-guarded, the supervised, the sacred. When selling, buyers he had met before were as cautious over the theft of their own goods as they were sharp-eyed to a bad deal. He had duped more than one of them in more than one way.

Yet for all of the torment the ghost caused him, it was Simon's companion, almost a friend, crouching beside him at the plague-victim gravesides, looking over his shoulder at the loot at the end of the day, riding behind him on the saddle in the rain. There was never any telling when the ghost boy would rise up in indignation and make Simon beg him for a reprieve, but he was there. Before Simon met MT, he had only the specter for company, and he had grown used to living with the mercurial ghost.

When he met Sister Mary Thomas, with her sage smoke and little cart, her black habit was still intact, but her rosary had irretrievably fallen into a grave a month ago. Her wimple was gone and though her hair had grown spikey and uneven, she still appeared to be a nun. He reasoned that she would provide him with an aura of legitimacy to mask his thieving. The forgiveness of God? Another fairy tale from the land of fools.

Simon and MT zig-zagged across the country, digging graves, pilfering bodies, reciting unbelieved and unheeded prayers. He commandeered a pony and hitched it to the cart, which MT thought was to relieve her of having to pull it but was really so he could steal heavier items.

One night around the fire Simon was drunk on ale and rummaging through his booty when he stretched his legs out and leaned back against a log.

"Sister Mary Thomas," he slurred. "MT. Empty. Fitting, don't you think?" he laughed. "Empty of husband and child. A virgin." He offered her the ale jug, which she refused. "Empty promises. You are Empty the Nun."

"Not amusing," she said, as she dug in the fire with the poker.

"Empty the None. Bride of none. Mother to none. Friend to none. Well maybe to me and that's as good as nothing." He took another big swig. "Home of none. Church of none. Prayers to none."

"That's blasphemy."

"Oh, come on, I see you! You don't pray before bed or stop for compline or the rest of them. You don't even pray over the dead anymore."

"You can't give last rites to the dead."

"Is that the reason?" He leaned forward and his face was hideous in the firelight. "I think it's because you're a believer in none."

She threw the poker down beside the fire and climbed under the cart to sleep. But she hadn't protested that he was wrong.

Now, at the manor house prison, Simon strained against the slats.

"What have we here? Did they call you...milady?" He flinched over the splintered gargoyle of her cap.

"Quiet," she whispered fiercely. MT pretended to inspect the men while considering her new dilemma: a second person who knew who she was. "I am here to do good," she said quietly.

"Oh, no longer empty of purpose?"

She looked for the sheriff, who was holding the horses in front. "I can make silence worth your while." She thought of the gold under the desk. He shook the slats of the corral.

"Sheriff," she called, "I need this one in the house."

"I need him for the jail," Baudwin protested.

"He won't be lounging on pillows here! I need a woodcutter." She returned to the sheriff who turned away from her.

"How many more of these…deliveries can I expect?" she said.

"The countryside is thin, that's certain, milady."

"Don't take them anywhere else," she commanded.

"This lot is for the earl."

Simon shook the slats again, but a guard charged forward and kicked his hands.

"It's very late for a…delivery," she said.

"We move on in the morning."

"They'll have to bed here in the barn. I have no blankets. As I said, my estate has been stripped bare in my absence. I'll send down a bucket of soup but that's all I can offer."

Baudwin bowed his head.

She strode to Simon's corral and checked that the sheriff was busy mustering his men and retrieving his own bedroll.

"What are you doing here?" she whispered to Simon.

"More to the point, what are *you* doing? Acting the lady!"

"I stumbled into it," she said, uncertain why she would want to explain herself to the likes of him. "What were the chances that there was another woman exactly my size. A portrait: we even look alike." *Except for the mole*, she thought.

"Pity," he said.

MT grabbed a sharpened hay fork from the back wall and jabbed it through the slats. Simon jumped back before he was impaled.

"The first thing to remember is that I am in charge here! I give the orders and whatever role I put you in, you work for me. Deference and obeisance, those are the only two attitudes you will display."

He didn't understand the fancy words, but the tines of the hay fork made it clear. "Understood," he said quickly.

She set the fork out of Simon's reach against the back wall.

"I shall collect this one in the morning," she barked at the sheriff.

Simon called to her as she headed back to the house. "Yes…milady!"

MT sputtered in indignation at the sound of his voice. When they were trudging through the countryside together, his complaints were incessant. The fruit wasn't ripe, or it was too ripe, the sun too hot, shade too broad, sundown too early, there were bugs or a chill. When he found a bow and arrow he announced that it was the crooked arrow's fault that he couldn't hit anything for their dinner. He was certain there were stones under his blanket even when they lay down in sand. The sweetest well water poured down the sides of his mouth as he drank it and just after he sighed in relief, he proclaimed that it contained too many minerals. MT stopped hearing the words of his relentless displeasure, just registered the buzz of it. Like insects, or the screech of an iron rake over boulders, the din of hinges breaking through rust. She left him when he killed the only sign of gaiety and joy they had encountered.

Two months into their journey, they had come across a bear

trainer and his two dogs who had captured a cub in the Black Forest and as the bear grew, they had crisscrossed Europe's fairs and ale houses, finally taking the massive animal in a boat across the channel to England. This bear trainer had rebelled against the tradition of staging bloody fights with the animals – dogs against the bear – and instead had choreographed a happy little maypole dance with them. The furry giant stood on his hind legs while the dogs circled him with ribbons in their mouths that were attached to the bear's hat. The trainer, in threadbare but still colorful vest and pants, squeaked out a jaunty tune on a reed flute. The bear would be crisscrossed with festive colors and at the climax the dogs would spin on their hind legs as well, all of them entwined with gay colors until the tune stopped. The animals dropped to all fours and the happy ribbons puddled around them. The trainer would doff a battered chapeaux for coins and applause.

When MT and Simon encountered them, they were camping at a crossroad unable to determine where there were any people left to enjoy their show and from the look of his lean-to and woodpile, the trainer had been indecisive for a while.

The trainer insisted on doing the show for free (though Simon grumbled about an ulterior motive), and MT clapped and laughed with pent-up delight. She was mesmerized by the seven-foot bear that towered over the trainer and the dogs, its lethal claws glinting in the sun, its head thrown back in an expression that seemed like joy, at odds with its deadly teeth. The dogs circling him pranced, lifting their paws and their heads. MT laughed that it was exhilarating to be frightened and delighted at once, to be drawn to gaiety and held back by fear. It was hard to remember days of gaiety, of young girls and May poles. After she smudged the trainer she invited him to join them for a meal and the two of them sat around the evening fire with the dogs, happy and relaxed. The bear laid down chained to a tree. Simon sat away from them in a thicket. He walked into the light of the fire to retrieve his dinner and disappeared again into the darkness.

Perhaps the lady should join them in their theater, the trainer said, go on the road with them. MT considered his offer. What she wouldn't give to spend the rest of her days doing something silly, to see clapping children, be surrounded by laughter during the day and curl up with the dogs at night. She dug her fingers into the dogs' fur. The bear trainer made suggestions for a route, told her of performances in the past. MT offered ideas of how she could help, things they might incorporate into the show.

In the morning, MT was chipper and bustled around making broth and caring for the dogs. The trainer wanted to show her the variations in their routine and try out some of her ideas. He strode through the crossroads introducing the show as if there was an audience, while the bear and the dog trotted into their places and began their circle dance.

MT smiled at the colors, the ribbons, the enchanting dogs and their dance.

But just as all the animals were on their back legs, bearing their chests, Simon stepped from behind a tree with his bow and a venomous smile, and shot an arrow through the bear's heart. It fell with a loud thud and a cloud of dust.

MT whirled around to see Simon's sneer.

The trainer let out a howl that MT had never heard even in the depth of the dying times, and he fell to his knees beside his beloved, motionless bear whose nose and mouth now leaked blood. The dogs stood rigidly, the ribbons at their feet now even more incongruous.

Simon shrugged his shoulders, though with less disdain than usual, and MT roared at him, then picked up a rock and hurled it at him. She pelted him with stones and the dogs took her cue and charged him until he climbed a tree a hundred yards away to avoid them.

MT railed at him from beneath the tree as the dogs jumped at the trunk. If he fell from the tree she would stand by and let the dogs do their worst. MT had barely been able to tolerate his cynical mutterings, but to kill an innocent!

"You just couldn't stand it, could you? Something silly. Something tender," she shouted. "If they had been fighters you would have…"

"If they had been fighters I would have wagered money," he said, looking down at her from the tree.

She turned back to the sobbing trainer whose face was blotchy, eyes and neck red as he sat in the dirt with his shoulders heaving. One of the dogs returned and licked the trainer's face and nose, though it didn't stop the tears. The trainer lay down beside the bear, his arm across the beast's chest, and one dog sat in the crook of the trainer's legs, standing guard.

Hours later, after Simon had been chased back up the tree

several times by the dogs, MT saw buzzards overhead and knew that wolves would be arriving soon.

"My good man," MT said quietly to the trainer, "we must leave him and flee. Your dogs will be no match for what arrives next, and you don't want to lose another member of your precious family."

"I will not leave him," the trainer vowed. "I will not."

MT wiped her own tears and considered what to do. As with a deer, if the bear was gutted, she could move the offal away from the carcass to divert the wolves. That at least would give them time, since digging a grave for an animal this large would take almost all day. She retrieved her hunting knife from the cart and the trainer gave his consent, though he turned away and called his dogs to him. MT carried the bear's guts to the tree that sheltered Simon, piling the bloody parts in a ring around the trunk. Let him be treed by a wolf pack, she thought. Let him be captive for days.

When she returned from depositing the last bit of offal, the trainer was using her knife to skin the bear. With choking sobs, he worked through the night scraping the hide as MT built a large fire and brought fresh water for the dog who flanked the man with her head on her paws, and to the dog under the tree. She started to dig.

Simon, silent for once, stayed in the branches. The trainer laid the huge hide over rocks in the morning sun and slept while it dried. MT continued the daunting task of digging a grave for the hapless dancer, hitched the pony to the carcass and, hours later when the grave was a large mound and she was dirty and exhausted, she gently woke the trainer. While holding the trainer's hand graveside, she prayed with an earnestness she had abandoned long ago. She made the trainer soup, though he wouldn't eat, and after dosing off, she woke to see him working on the pelt. As the sun set, he wrapped himself in it. They had grown up together, he explained, souls ripped from the forest and the hearth, trying to be kind in a bloodied world. The dog nestled her nose deep in the bear's fur.

When MT woke to bank the fire in the night, the trainer was remarkably still and MT chose not to disturb his sleep, but in the morning he was dead, stiff and pale. The dogs had run into the forest, and both Simon and the pony were nowhere to be found.

MT sat on her haunches and wept doubled over, then dug the trainer a grave. She couldn't part with the pelt, though. She clutched it to her, a *memento mori* and she fell into an exhausted sleep, entirely enrobed by the bearskin.

Simon, on the road with the pony, had been shocked by the trainer's grief like few things had ever shocked him. In his experience, men with a dry eye killed horses who had carried them into battle and chased away dogs who had been at their side for years. The trainer's weeping was poetry from a fish. *Didn't they understand? He couldn't let her go. Couldn't have MT, the little stump of a nun, go off with happy dogs and silly ribbons, leaving him with no one but the ghost.*

It wasn't that he was heartless, Simon reasoned. MT hadn't been aware during their journey together that Simon had been weaving small dolls out of ferns and depositing them on the bodies of everyone they buried. A wordless, heartfelt devotion, he had left one on the pillow of his mother before he left. In the graves, he surreptitiously slipped one into a mother's hand or set two upon a mother and child, sometimes one near the ear of a man in the hopes it would whisper some comfort. Every pilfered fruit cart, every mantle robbed of an heirloom received a fern doll in return. Before he met MT he wove them in front of the fire at night but with her he waited until she had climbed under the cart to sleep.

In the months following the death of the giant dancer, though, all his fern creations were bears and he set them under trees in the woods, beside a creek, wedged in rocks in a dale. He wove hundreds of bears, left one on a pillow in brothels, on a bench in ale houses, at the blacksmith, and along fence posts of abandoned farms.

After the bear's death, MT stayed in the crossroads for six days hoping the dogs might return. She kept the pelt as a reminder of how close she had come to having a life of gaiety and she slept rolled into its heartbreak. On the sixth day, she lashed two branches to the front of the cart to turn the bearskin into a tent and she lined the cart bed with sweetgrass and sage, calling to the dogs, then finally moving on alone and disappointed with the smoking censer in front. At night she clutched the bear's claws, as if the smooth, black, lethal defense gave her strength.

Now Simon was here at the manor house, destined to scratch

the shine off of everything, at best. And the knowledge he held could be the death of her.

I will not give this place up, she thought, when the sheriff moved the prisoners on in the morning, and Simon sat alone in the cell. She remembered both the devotion of Claudia to her child and the bearskin pelt as a refusal to surrender the dead.

CHAPTER SIX

The horse of Percy's epiphany had been attached to a flatbed wagon and while trying to get at a trough of water and the pasture beyond it had gotten wedged into the gate, unable to get to either. The horse was dusty, dehydrated, with dried foam around its mouth from days of struggling to get free. The horse's ribs protruded from its side, and judging by the shabby wagon, it had never been anything but a peasant's nag. Its whinny was weak, and it barely raised its head when Percy commanded his dogs to sit as he cautiously approached the animal. From the look of the bloodied sores on the horse's back, it had been harnessed for so long that the leather had rubbed the poor animal raw.

"Easy now." He scowled over the pus-coated sores. "We'll get you out."

Percy climbed the fence and filled a bucket with water for the horse. "Slowly now. Easy. Little at a time." It shuffled when Percy took the bucket of water away, but he knew from the stable boys that a horse was just dumb enough to make itself sick with too much water.

Step one would be to tie the horse so it wouldn't bolt, Percy knew. Securing it to the fence, Percy struggled to unpin the wagon, the hardware bent and twisted from the horse's struggle. After every few minutes of banging on the hitch, Percy stopped and offered the horse more water. Build its strength, he thought. He could do little to quell its fear, but he could strengthen it to withstand what it couldn't comprehend. He talked to the horse. He talked to his dogs. Pulling the last pin out of the wagon hitch, Percy leapt back, knowing that the sudden freedom would make the horse bolt and thankfully the gate post was strong enough to withstand the pivoting horse.

Blood had dried the leather of the harness to the horse's hide and would hurt it further if removed now so the horse would have to continue in the chafing harness until Percy could warm enough water to soak off the blood. Percy knew that the horse wanted nothing more than to lie down, but it would roll on its wounds, so he hammered a post into a patch of grass to tether it in the paddock. The horse walked slowly, head bent, unable to muster the strength to even shake its mane.

He built a fire, warmed the bucket of water and when it seemed that the horse had eaten enough grass, he poured the warm water over the wounds, loosening the leather, stopping to calm the horse, beginning again. It wasn't until the sun was setting that he was finally able to free the last bit of scab and, with one last plaintive whinny from the horse, pull the harness free. Percy stood back as the horse trotted weakly around the post. Percy wouldn't untie it, though. The sun was setting, and an animal with open wounds would invite wolves if it ran free into the forest.

He called his dogs to him and sent the ratters into a small barn on the property to frighten away any vermin. After they returned, he led the horse inside, stationed the fighting dogs at the doors, a hunting dog at each window and kept the ratters with him. Percy let go of the reins and the horse slowly trod the perimeter of the building while Percy laid straw in a corral. He led the horse into the corral and, speaking in soothing tones, removed the bit from its mouth, watching his fingers as the animal protested. It collapsed into the bedding and Percy reasoned that even if it died that night at least it would be at peace. A small voice offered him a bit of solace as well: he may be unskilled and dependent, but he knew enough to save a horse.

Taking the largest fighting dog with him in case of wolves, Percy went into the abandoned garden and pulled up carrots, turnips and parsnips that had grown unattended, stripped beans and peas, plucked apples and pears. He and the dogs ate heartily of the pheasant the hunting dog had brought him the day before. As he did every night, he took inventory of himself: he felt fine, but if he died in the night the dogs and the horse would starve in the barn if he closed the door, but if he left the door open the wolves might amass and while his fighters were fierce, they would be no match for a large pack. It was a chance he had to take so he stationed the fighters at the open door and slept with a sense of resignation: even if he died before dawn, he had made it farther than most.

In the morning, he found that the smallest dogs were curled up with the horse, having licked its wounds to help them heal and he was glad for the comfort they had given. But when they got ready to go, leaving the barn open so the horse could roam, the horse stood up and followed them. Percy pivoted on his heel to wave the horse back but then thought better of it. There was no one around to care for it: he hadn't encountered another person in days.

But more surprisingly, he wondered about himself. Why shouldn't he be a man who had a horse? Perhaps his life didn't have to be confined to shoveling out dog kennels for a lord's pleasure. In this world nearly emptied of people, why couldn't he be prosperous in his own right? Not a servant to the baron, or any gentry. *That's not possible,* he thought. *He is a dog-boy who knows nothing.*

The horse followed.

An hour later he encountered a flock of stupefied sheep clustered in the middle of the road, and though his dogs were not herders, the sheep didn't know that. *Why not have sheep,* he thought, though he had to be stern with his dogs to keep them from treating the animals like prey. The sheep were marshalled down the road without too much resistance and he felt more like a farmer with every step. Who was there to stop him from settling into the largest farm he could find?

And yet a voice inside him reminded him that he was just Percy of the Hounds. He had *watched* the farmer and her family. He didn't actually know anything. His mother had spent a lifetime shoveling salt and died broken, just as he would die after a lifetime of shoveling after dogs. He abandoned a few sheep who wandered off because he couldn't leave the rest of his livestock unattended, and he didn't know how to round them up again anyway. Wrong kind of dog, he told himself.

Surely he could farm under these conditions, he told himself. Tree nuts were like gravel under his feet. Courgettes now blanketing the ground were touched by pendulous clusters of oversized grapes. Without hunters, the grouse were thick under foot, partridges moved in great flocks and deer clustered in growing herds. Pigs not reclaimed from their annual free-range feast in the woods had amassed in such numbers that they became even more self-assured and dangerous. In some places, wolves had so much to eat that they had grown in number but had lost their ferocity and could be seen bored and lounging in the afternoon sun. Fish crowded the ponds for the taking. Cows kept their calves. Goats cavorted with badgers and foxes in the cottages where the empty beds of those who had milked and corralled and butchered them became excellent nests and caves.

As the sun started setting on his slow journey westward, he decided to take shelter in a small farm by the road. He drove his livestock into a barn while the dogs sat around him awaiting orders. He thought the animals seemed relieved to be indoors but couldn't be sure. What if he took over this farm? No. He was Percy, Stealer of Livestock. Not true, said another voice. Gathered from others who are gone. Rescued. He was Percy, Owner of a Horse. Percy, Keeper of Sheep. Wasn't he now a tenant farmer, not a servant? He tore the baron's patch off his vest but slept in the barn.

He was there more than a month but continued living in the barn. While he reasoned that the house was still too close to sickness and death it was really that the house felt like someone else's. He woke to birdsong and blooming fruit trees, a gentle life. His solitude was the only indication that death had run through the country. The horror of the plague seemed to be behind them.

One morning, he stretched his arms as he walked to the fence and regarded the paddock covered with a low-hanging fog. First to catch his eye was one of his fighting dogs, panting, with blood covering its muzzle. Looking out at the paddock, he saw blotches of white and red like giant mushrooms and when he realized what they were, he jumped over the fence and crisscrossed the field to find six of his sheep gutted by the dogs. *Any fool would have known to keep his dogs in line*, he thought.

Percy locked the fighters in a tool shed because they were now driven by blood lust. There were muzzles for them at the manor but that did him no good now. He burned the sheep carcasses, watching the pyre with resignation. He thought he would have more time to learn how to butcher sheep and he had no clue how to skin them. There was no point in staying, really, though he knew the fault was his, not the farm's. He couldn't live in the barn when the weather turned, and maybe he could carry tools and supplies in a goat cart that was in the grasses nearby. He strapped the fighters to the goat cart and got back on the road in the morning with his reduced flock and his dogs.

He found another farm, this one close to the road with a

stream, and the evening chill encouraged him to move into the house. Thankfully, it was a mild winter, and the grass grew for the livestock. There were only a few days when he had to break ice off the rain barrel and trough for the horse. Percy spent weeks in front of the fire making a bow and crafting arrows and the first time he took the hunting dogs out they bagged enough pheasant for Percy to smoke, though he mangled the flesh with the first two. He took the fighting dogs out to hunt venison just to maintain both their skills and their obedience and though his butchering job started out clumsy and wasted meat it improved as he progressed. His hands became callous and weather-beaten.

Sitting in front of the fire that night, he thought about his life and what he wanted. Before the Great Mortality, it hadn't been an open question, but now that there was no one in his way, he was free to add to the list. Land, he knew, and a wife, a family.

At the manor, most of the kennel hands were old bachelors who had settled into the barracks. Three years ago, when one of the men in his twenties married a village woman and moved to her family's farm, the kennel hands treated him as if he were walking to the Far East. It was a brave endeavor, they told him, then predicted his demise, and poured into the village pub to drink themselves stupid. The baron had to send a wagon to pick them all up and for several days they pretended that their sorrow was a hangover. Then they excused their lethargy by saying they were heartbroken to see their colleague go, but as it crept into their minds that they actually regretted the life they had chosen, when they realized that they had let that opportunity slip by, they reverted to their bawdy denunciation of marriage and boasted of their sexual exploits.

That wouldn't be him, Percy told himself, and recited his list of desires: land and a family.

A week later there was a knock on the door and Percy didn't open it. He crept around the side of the cottage and called out to the visitor. It was a robust older man who raised his hand in greeting and, while they inspected each other for signs of sickness, they chatted about their travels, of what they had seen on the road, of the quietude. They walked six feet apart to the paddock and regarded the sheep and the visitor gave him advice on how to protect his garden from frost, how to combine plants to put life back into the soil. Percy needed chickens to keep the bugs down, the old man said. Percy invited him to stay but the man insisted on sleeping in the barn, which made both of them feel easier. Percy locked the fighters into the tool shed again and brought the rest of the dogs into the house.

Percy woke up feeling hopeful. Here was someone who could teach him what he needed to know, and it surprised him how much the company and conversation had cheered him.

He let the dogs loose and walked toward the barn with a glass of apple juice he had pressed for his guest. The dogs started barking and Percy turned the corner to see that the visitor was not in the barn and that half of his sheep were gone. He pivoted on his heel and slammed the cup to the ground. Thankfully, the horse was in the paddock standing between the gate and the rest of the sheep. Apparently this is what happens when you have something of value, he thought. As a man who had had nothing it was new to him.

The farm was too near a crossroads, he decided. This was clearly not the place to stay, he resolved, so he headed west again the following week.

On the road, he cut himself a switch and gathered up a dairy cow and her calf without wondering if they were trapped. Now he wasn't Percy the Rescuer. At noon he ran himself ragged trying to catch a couple of chickens but told himself he didn't have a cage for them anyway. He wasn't hard-hearted enough to hitch the horse to another wagon when he found one. Instead, he just dug up saplings and tied them across the horse's back. In the following weeks random sheep were added to the flock. He kept walking, telling himself that the next farm where they stopped had not been large enough. The dogs carried saddle bags filled with vegetables and herbs that he hoped could be transplanted into a garden and he struggled to remember which went into the shade and which into the sun. He had dug them up without noticing. The next farm was too large, he decided after resting there for a week. He scavenged good tools when he found a cart and a harness for the fighting dogs. Sacks of seed, though he couldn't tell for what, went into the back. The next week the farm was too far away from a creek, and the following week, the barns leaned too much, the following day it was not on a path to a market.

It had been slow going because he was now shepherding another large flock of sheep plus the horse and the slow-moving cow who stopped to suckle her calf, but when he rounded the corner he realized that he was now at the farm at the base of the manor hill, just across the bridge from the main road, the very farm he had studied from afar for years. He stopped in the middle of the road. Why had he walked this far? Why had he ruled out every farm along the way? Now all of his livestock would be seized by the baron, and Percy, through his indecision, had willingly walked back into a position of servitude. His dogs became lively at returning home, but he kept them in check by his side. Maybe the baron would allow him to rent the land, which at least was a step up from being a dog tender. It would be a bargain that bettered him. Perhaps the baron would be generous, he thought, then scoffed at the idea. The baron was selfish and greedy, and his wife was legendary for her cruelty. People avoided her. They stiffened and looked straight ahead, he was told, supposedly because of a demonic cap she wore. The smallest of his dogs trembled so fiercely at her approach that he usually kept them in their kennels whenever the Master of the Hounds was asked to present the dogs at a formal event.

He got the sheep, cow, calf and horse into a paddock, peered into the windows of the farmhouse where he dropped the improvised saddlebags and resolved to climb the hill to ask the baron's permission to farm. But he stopped between the cottage and the road, unwilling to proceed. The baron knew him as a simple tender of dogs. He had no belief in Percy's ability to be responsible for livestock and a voice inside Percy's head told him that he, himself, had no confidence in his ability, either. But there was a desire. Why couldn't he? Why shouldn't he?

Jess Wells

He paced up and down the length of the cottage, out to the overgrown garden and back, wondering if he should gather all the livestock and move down the road to another farm that was more hidden and whose ownership would be less obvious. The baron and baroness wouldn't recognize him, of course: he was always so far back in any display of servants and tenders that he could see the feather in the cap of the Master of the Hounds but little else. He had only been inside the house once, as the baron invited only servants of high rank to the Christmastime Yule celebration. Perhaps the baron didn't know of him as his dog boy. He looked at the dark patch where the baron's coat of arms had been and took off his coat. Perhaps Percy could pass himself off as just an ordinary man and since so many had died and there were so few to tend to the livestock and work the fields, maybe the baron would be happy to take him on in a different position.

But Percy was not talking about being a different sort of servant or staff. He wanted something more. Agency over his own life, some path to prosperity. A hide, acreage enough to support a family. A burgage he could rent from a lord. He walked into the cottage and sat on a dusty chair with his head in his hands. His mother, God rest her soul, would have been so proud of him and so comfortable in a cottage like this instead of dying in the salt fields and the shack where she had lived. She could have sat at this solid table, tended these curtains, embroidered by the fire. And what about his dogs? Because they *were* his dogs now. On the road they had provided meals for him, alerted him to danger and had curled up with him as a pack under trees in the rain. Was he now expected to turn them over, give them back? He would be sad to see his dogs go, but there was nothing for it. He doubted the baron would remember that they were his dogs unless told and it was said the baroness beat her wolfhound, kept it chained to her bed at night, and just as bad, kept it apart from the other dogs, denying it life in a clan. On the few occasions he had seen it, it broke his heart to see how skittish and afraid the animal was. No, the dogs would stay here while he approached the manor house, though they were always at his side. He would return them if requested. But only if requested. An omission wasn't really a lie, was it? And the livestock was not really the duke's, having been gathered from all points along his journey. His thoughts were racing: the baron couldn't claim ownership just because an animal was on his land, or any ewe walking down the road could be seized. He was offering a valuable service, and it was reasonable to want something in return, wasn't it? As he paced in the cottage, he was tempted to just tend his livestock and settle into the house, to just wait for someone's protest, but he thought better of it: that was a line he would not cross. He shut the dogs in the barn with the horse. He was a man in his own right, energized by his conviction, and he would demand recognition.

Percy could tell that the boy standing sentry above the front gate was not from the manor because he innocently asked Percy his name. Percy had always been called Percy of the Hounds. He was at a loss.

"Percy... Hounder. Percy Hounder."

The boy clambered down from the parapet to alert the baroness.

MT strode across the courtyard gripping a long staff, her other hand on the hilt of a knife in her belt. She ordered that the door be opened and all stood yards away from Percy. "Good day to you. State your business."

Percy bowed to her and removed his cap. She was as short and wide as the legends said but he was surprised that the glass on the infamous cap danced in the sunlight.

"I am requesting permission of the baron to farm, to rent the burgage …at the base of the hill."

"The baron, God rest his soul, fell from the sickness, as have so many, and I carry on in his stead."

"I am sorry for your loss, milady, and will pray for his lordship's soul."

"I thank you. Are you... familiar with the landscape?" Had he been here before? "You have… experience?"

"I have a reasonably sized flock of sheep, milady, and a dairy cow with calf that I have driven for many miles. As well as saplings and seedlings." He omitted the dogs from the inventory.

"Dairy would be a very welcome addition to our larder." MT smiled.

The smile took him off guard. It had no trace of the cruelty and viciousness for which she was known. Had it been just a legend?

Then Percy's fear tightened his shoulders. The baroness's wolfhound trotted in the gate, and seeing Percy, bounded up like a puppy to lick his hands. The elkhound had twigs knotted in its fur and blood dried around its muzzle, but it had a sparkle in its eyes that Percy had never seen. Fat, happy and free, it had lived in the woods and eaten the quail that had bred without harvest or hunter. It rubbed its head against Percy's hand but then turned and saw MT. The dog started trembling and withdrew behind Percy's legs.

MT recognized the elkhound from the portrait. (*The dog had been left behind, monstrous woman!*) But then she realized that the dog knew the man and the man, the dog. This was no stranger looking for a farm. This was a man who knew the baron. The dog rubbed its face across Percy's pants and Percy, convinced that his identity as a dog boy was about to be blown, gave it a quick rub around the ears and shoved it away.

MT knew her charade was under threat: a dog cannot be fooled by dresses and caps. If she had been free to be herself, MT would have greeted it with warmth and tousled its head. But the baroness was cruel to all so MT squared her shoulders and clicked her fingers, commanding the animal to her side. It responded and took the spot as it had in the portrait, sniffed her hand and registered a difference, then pushed its nose right up against the dress and trembled.

Smile or not, Percy thought, *the dog's fear made it plain: this was definitely the baroness*. He was thirsty after his long journey and disoriented by the indecision bouncing around his head. "May I... trouble you for a sip of water?" He raised his hand toward the well at the corner of the property but withdrew his hand quickly: his gesture showed that he knew the layout of the manor and so was another clue to his previous servitude. Her cap showed him fragments of a man: shifting bits with no pattern.

MT stiffened and then curtly nodded her head, alerted to his knowledge of both the dog and the property and she pointed to the same corner. The baroness's elkhound slunk into the house.

MT turned her face away from him as he smoothly brought up the bucket and dipped in the ladle. She accompanied him back to the gate and down the hill as far as the prison corral, though neither spoke. There were now two men who held dangerous knowledge. *But the poor dog*, she thought. *It shouldn't have to be afraid.* She would ask the maids to air out her dresses tomorrow and hang them with sprigs of rosemary and lavender.

~ * ~ * ~ * ~

After watching Percy return to the farm, MT paced back and forth in front of Simon's corral, glad that the sheriff was gone, and she searched the ground for reassurance. She had several gold coins in a hidden pocket and was considering her options. Simon was a thief by trade, entirely driven by money. A dishonorable man, she grumbled to herself, remembering his slaughter of the gentle bear. But the manor needed supplies, and she wasn't going into any village or town for fear of discovery. And no baroness shops for herself. She presumed that if Simon thought there was more gold to be earned, he might buy supplies and return.

"We're doing good work here," she began, but stopped the explanation as she had never known him to be motivated to do the right thing. "I need supplies to reinvigorate the manor and employ all these people. Would you be interested in going into town and securing them? I will want a thorough accounting when you return because, while I will reward you for your time and effort, I will not tolerate your skimming off the top, do you understand?" She drew out a gold coin. "There is more, some of it for you."

He got on his knees and leaned forward to inspect it. "Very good...milady." He bowed more to avoid his reflection in her cap than out of deference.

"I am the baroness and while I have been hard-hearted and cruel in the past, the death I have witnessed has softened my heart. Do you understand? The baron is dead, taken by the sickness, but I am committed to carrying on." She opened the corral and stood in front of him, wondering what evil she was unleashing. "Can you do this?"

"Happy to be of service...milady."

She hissed close to his ear. "I will take you down if you betray me." *Or if you let all these women be recaptured*, she thought, *if you make all these fine people destitute. Or kill what little happiness we have created here.*

She stormed back toward the manor house but each step into her domain calmed her. Hallways had fresh sweetgrass on the floors. Jacob was sitting next to the fire, explaining something about Queen Matilda to the youngest girls who were enchanted with him. When MT turned the corner, she beamed at him. All scrambled to their feet to curtsy and before he bowed Jacob smiled at her as if she was sweets on Sunday. This was joy, she thought, caring for people who mattered and listening to the whimsy of a dear young man.

~ * ~ * ~ * ~

Simon returned the following day driving a horse and wagon filled with casks and boxes, pots and pans, chairs and bolts of cloth. The maids excitedly rushed toward the wagon, grabbed the goods but grew silent and downcast when they saw Simon.

"You there!" Gertrude called to him as she charged across the courtyard. "Bring me more knives and any spices you can find. And flour: wheat, spelt, rye, anything."

"There's no flour anywhere. Of any kind. The bishop's mill is broken."

Gertrude shook her head and grumbled. "Never thought I'd wish for a bishop." Even with this delivery they would still be eating in shifts, and he hadn't brought a spit for roasting, so she was still confined to stew. Rabbit stew.

It didn't take long for the staff to steer clear of Simon: shortly after arriving he had complained about the food and so was not welcome in the kitchen even though he brought them badly needed tools. They pushed a bowl of stew toward him and sent him on his way. He scoffed in the face of the little sentry boy so the old man had Simon wait at the gate in the hopes he would catch a chill. Simon had looked Claudia up and down as if she was a giant and she ordered the women to be wary.

MT had a room made up for him next to the room with the old man and orphan boy, as far away from her library as possible. She would have locked him out of the main house if she could have. She ordered him to show her the remaining money from this first journey, which was scant, and she glared at him then pressed another coin into his hand with instructions to leave again first thing in the morning to buy more. Simon was too transfixed by the gold to protest though he narrowed his eyes and wondered what game she was playing.

MT ordered the seamstresses to start first on bedclothes with the new cloth that Simon brought, with a plan to move to shawls for the women, and someday, MT pronounced, wall hangings to keep out the damp.

Claudia glared at her: they were better off with heavy capes and bedrolls for a quick get-away. Still shocked over the gold, Claudia stayed as far away from MT as she could, leaving rooms when MT entered, distancing her from this theft, though not moving from MT's bedroom because it would break with custom. This wasn't just an egg or a pie from a farmer, it was enough of a royal's gold to change the lives of an entire village. She could search under the desk to find the bag but the thought of being responsible for that crime made her feel faint. She should leave while she could, even if she left without any gold at all. She knew she wouldn't though. Just a few coins would make it possible to restart her family's farm and ensure a decent life for her and Daisy.

Despite the chilly relations between MT and Claudia though, the manor house was brightened by the women's chatter as they sewed, and others worked in the kitchen as it grew better equipped with each wagon load. The servants' table had enough plates, bowls and spoons. Sleeping two in each bed, there were enough blankets to go around. They sat in the afternoon sun and hemmed bedding, then chatted brightly as they decided to begin on a cloth for the head table.

"Shall we embroider your initials," they asked MT, and she tried not to look stumped by the question.

"Let's do flowers," MT said, trying to recover. "My husband's name…" she looked down as if from grief and shook her head. The maids turned back to the task, quietly devising a combination of blossoms and vines.

In the morning, Claudia and MT walked along an overgrown path that ran along the base of the hill on which the warren lodge was perched. They were united in an effort to find a route that all the women could use for escape. They needed something that didn't run by the main road or past the jail.

"This discussion isn't over, you know," Claudia said sternly, thinking of both the gold and MT's plans to remain. MT did not reply.

Families of quail scurried in front of them, and they took stock of overgrown blackberry bushes and laden pear trees.

"These will make excellent jam," MT started but looked up at Claudia and stopped. More long-term plans. Better kept to herself.

Claudia glanced down at her but kept her face placid. Despite her outrage at the gold, there was something she liked about this bold and odd little woman. *No shrinking violet, this one.*

The pig pens and horse paddocks were empty but as they parted the overgrown branches of a walnut grove, they stepped into a small field of barley and sighed with relief. The first step toward bread, though the bishop's mill was not operational.

"There should be a shed halfway up the field," Claudia said, and they marched toward it. Sickles and scythes, twine, hay rakes, threshing sieves hung neatly, untouched. "Apparently of no interest to thieves," Claudia said but turned to find that MT was no longer in the shed.

"What is that?" MT asked her when Claudia joined her outside.

"What is what?"

"That. Glinting. A window?"

"I don't know." Claudia was perplexed. "I've never seen it."

MT closed the doors, and they strode toward the enigma.

It was a stone cottage, solid, with ornately carved shutters and door. They pulled back fast-growing ivy and branches that had been purposely placed to obscure it. Only Claudia was tall enough to see in the high windows. She was expecting a shepherd's hut but stepped back from what she saw.

"What? What is it?" MT asked and stood on her tiptoes, still not nearly tall enough.

They forced open the door then stopped in awe: tufted pillows, fine upholstery, a rabbit fur cover on a bed with an ornately carved headboard and a wide chair. There were tapestries on the wall, fine linens on the bed. Goblets and pewter plates. Porcelain figurines and a place setting for two.

"A love nest for the baron?" Claudia suggested. "I had no idea."

"No." MT lifted a fur-trimmed robe from a chair. She held it in front of her. It was her size. "For the baroness," she said.

Claudia was dumbstruck.

"Claudia, we need to see this baby."

Claudia reluctantly scooped the baby from the sling and cooed to her, held her under her arms and let her legs unfold to the table. MT ran her hands down the baby's legs to straighten them.

"So, she will be tall," MT said. "Does she have hair?"

"Not much," Claudia said and as the two women held their breath, she removed the cap from the baby's head.

"It's blond! The baron's hair is…"

"Dark," said Claudia, remembering the stink of it as he bent over her breasts. They looked around the cottage and back to the child.

Claudia dropped her nose into the down on Daisy's head and inhaled deeply. No wonder they hadn't recorded it in the family bible. No wonder there had been no celebration. She was not only a girl, but the outcome of a tryst! Still a mystery, though: who on earth could have tolerated that loathsome toad of a woman, the real baroness? Who would creep into that cottage, well-appointed though it was? Apparently the baron had no inkling of the baby's origin or perhaps the baroness, dead before the child's hair had grown in, was waiting to see if she could get away with it and pass the child off as legitimate.

Claudia danced the baby across the tabletop. No record, no claim, no threat. Now that Daisy was both an orphan and born on the wrong side of the sheets she was a dream come true. A child of her own. *Her* sweet child. The thought of it brought milk flooding into Claudia's breasts. She put her daughter onto her nipple and rocked them both with relief.

As she deftly switched the baby to the other breast, though, the nagging fear returned. The parents were dead, that was true. A child with blonde hair would look more like her than the Duchess: true also. No relatives would come to claim her, assuming any had survived the Great Mortality. But there was a man out there, a blonde man, who had more rights to Daisy than she did, and his lurking presence made her shudder so hard that her nipple popped out of the baby's mouth. The child looked up in surprise.

"Not to worry, little one," she lied as she brought the nipple back to the baby's lips. She feigned a smile. "Mommy has this in hand. All is well."

But it wasn't. Somewhere there was a man, probably a lord, with designs on her child. If he knew about her. If he cared. If he was alive. If he didn't assume that his bastard girl was dead with the rest.

If discovered, she recited to herself, she was the wet nurse. She was tending to the child. Protecting the child against kidnappers and slavers. Her position of authority in the household could be explained, perhaps exalted, even rewarded. She was making no claims of being gentry, and if she kept her hands off the gold, she could easily slip back into her previous life. As soon as she thought it, though, she knew it wasn't true. She would not give Daisy up, even if it was to the kindest member of the baroness's family. Not to anyone. She made silent plans to store a parcel for the two of them, ready for their escape into the woods if her possession of the baby was challenged. She would not give her up.

CHAPTER SEVEN

Claudia was supervising the final trim on the cloth for the high table knowing that it wasn't practical for women trying to flee but that it would be the first thing after bedding that a baroness would request. Suddenly, she remembered the flash of blonde hair on the man who had asked to take over the farm.

He was not a random stranger, MT had said, he was someone who had lived here before, a blonde, potentially lover of the baroness and so the rightful father of Daisy. It sent panic through Claudia. Just yesterday, she had finally agreed to allow Daisy to spend her days with the other infants and toddlers in a room by the kitchen. All that morning, she had been nervous, her arms felt empty, and her chest seemed suddenly exposed. But there was work to be done to keep all of these people fed and warm and she had volunteered to be the chief of staff, so she had reluctantly turned Daisy over to the care of others.

Now realizing the danger, Claudia walked to the library as fast as she could without raising suspicion.

MT agreed. "Definitely. He knows the property, has been here, has met the baroness. On the other hand, he has a cow, and we could do with some dairy in our community."

"Community?" Claudia was pacing in front of the desk, incensed. "This is not an abbey! We are not building a community; we are trespassing on someone else's property. Oh, and," she said with sarcasm and pointedness, "that someone is the king!"

"Well, it won't do to make this visitor an enemy by refusing his request," MT countered. "Besides, if he was the previous farmer he would just settle back into the place, which means that he is perhaps as much of an imposter as you and me."

"But you've agreed to let him stay? How could you do that? You must send him away!"

"On what grounds?"

"You don't need grounds, or reasons, or even logic! You are the lady of the manor." *This woman's inability to understand power, let alone to act like a lady, was infuriating,* Claudia thought.

"Do you recognize him?" MT asked.

"I have only been here since just before the birth of the child and now we know why the baron and baroness hid me. I met a few chambermaids, rarely even the kitchen staff. The point is though, that there is a very good chance that this man is Daisy's father." She was suddenly even more panicked. "I should retrieve her."

"Calm yourself," MT said. "It would be very odd for a woman of your standing to constantly walk around with a baby on her chest. Besides, she needs to grow up around other children."

"Again," Claudia said as she leaned on the desk, "you are acting as if we will be here for years! The hangman will arrive before she learns to walk, let alone before she interacts with other children. You must send this… farmhand away! Refuse him!" Claudia dropped her head into her hands. "We now have two men who know that you are an impostor, one of whom could lay claim to my child, and the other who has an inkling of the fortune."

"Plus, we are stealing from the sheriff, the king and the bishop," MT said.

"Then I join you in your plea: God, let our deaths be swift."

Despite Claudia's misgivings, though, MT could not remember ever being so happy. The manor house was enlivened, there was laughter from the kitchens. They were safe behind the walls (hopefully). Protected (to a degree). There was an efficiency here and her leadership gave her a sense of well-being. To care for others. To orchestrate and arbitrate. To devise solutions. She relished the beauty of a plan. Here was the flock she had always wanted but assumed she could never have, even before the Great Mortality. Being the head of a convent required obedience and religious fervor, both of which were anathema to her now. But here it was different. The stronger she was, the more protection she could give.

MT had been on the receiving end of orders her entire life and most times the instructions had baffled her. Sent to the well when the cistern was closer. Made to dig for tubers when she could see they weren't fully formed. The nuns ordered to stay praying on their knees while the rain poured through untended shutters. The first abbess was from royalty and knew nothing of crops, so they planted too late in the season, hosted a large group of priests who ate through their larder, and the women went hungry in the winter. That summer the abbess wouldn't allow the nuns to harvest the apple crop because of Eve's sin, though it was their largest orchard, and the rats had a feast instead. The second abbess insisted that nothing be done without her permission and then rode back to her father's castle to feast while the nuns were too cowed to even cook. It seemed that in a nun's life, the less successful, malnourished and threadbare, the better. To fail seemed to be a form of devotion. The vow of poverty became a pledge of incompetence, it seemed, while the surrounding village that could have benefited from good, strong crops out of the generous acreage the abbey controlled became hungry and impoverished as well. More than once, MT had been locked away with nothing but water for making tiny suggestions, discussing the commands with others in the garden or muttering alternate plans under her breath. The sin of pride, of rebellion, the abbess intoned at prayers, and made MT lay prostrate in front of her while all the nuns watched. No matter how MT couched it, how obsequious and self-effacing she was when offering her opinion, it wound up with her locked in her cell, made to scrub the muck buckets until she gagged or digging rows in the frozen ground until her hands were blue. Despite it all it didn't stop her from silently inventing a different process nor did it dampen her imagination, but she had longed to find space for her ideas and her voice. Her late-night whisperings with the innovative nun kept her from feeling crazy but not from being frustrated. One Sunday when the oldest nun pulled her back inside out of the snow and worked to heal her near-frozen hands, MT changed her silent prayers. "Mary, Mother of God save us from waste. Save us from power that has no purpose. Bless us in our rebellion against the uncaring, unfeeling, and the stupid."

She would do it a different way when she was abbess, she had pledged, but the loss of her faith jettisoned that plan and any opportunity for leadership, it seemed. Until now. Until being someone else.

In the morning Claudia was resolved: the best way through this problem was to head straight at it and send this blonde man packing before he even saw the baby. With her shoulders thrown back and her spine stiff, she headed down the hill to the farm of the blonde interloper.

If he was the father she intended to take Daisy and run as far and fast as she could. Let him try to stop her, she growled to herself. She would wrestle in the mud to best him.

Tight, angry, and ready to fight, Claudia was completely unmasked by the breadth of Percy's smile as he hurried across the paddock, opened the gate and held it as she entered.

"A beautiful day, is it not?" Percy said. "If you stand here," as he gestured to a plank of wood at the fence, "you may keep your shoes from getting muddy." He held out his hand to steady her as Claudia lifted her skirts a bit and stepped onto the plank. She did it tentatively, unaccustomed to such consideration. "How may I be of..." He caught himself: a farmer does not offer service. "What brings you to my... humble farm?"

"To...send you on your way," she said sternly, but her heart softened when she saw how his shoulders dropped. Such beautiful hair, like summer wheat. Her hand in his. But he had to go.

He looked at the ground. "I don't understand. The baroness welcomed me, gave me permission."

Claudia fumbled for an explanation as she withdrew her hand. A house manager could not over-rule a baroness but as she floundered, Percy's dogs rounded the corner of the barn in formation: the fighters, the hunters, then ratters as if at a military parade, and they trotted toward the two of them.

"Aren't those the..." Claudia began.

Percy rubbed his forehead and looked at the ground. "Yes. They are the baron's dogs and if the baroness insists on having them... I have no intention of stealing anything." He shuffled with anxiety. He had destroyed his own plan by returning. Percy the Fool. "You lived here as well, then. To have recognized the dogs."

"Only seen through the window at a summer fete."

"She has allowed me to be the tenant on this farm, hasn't she?"

"I believe she has, but how do you come to have the baron's dogs?" He was her height but trim, muscled, and she should have known he was not a farmer from the pallor and smoothness of his skin. She could see why the baroness would have taken him to bed. Anyone would. No matter how she felt about him, though, she needed Daisy's parentage determined. "Who are you, really?"

Believing that all was lost, and that it would be just hours before this farm and its livestock was taken from him, he told her of his years of service in the baron's kennels, how the dogs followed him on his flight to the coast to find his mother, their slow walk back and the many farms. Though he had no reason to trust her, it spilled out of him. He told her of freeing the horse and there was hunger in his voice as he explained his desire to better himself, to seize the opportunity, the plea to be understood, the hope that she would agree. Or that at least she would keep all this to herself.

"It's a blessing to have this chance," he said. "A chance to grow something, have something of one's own. A flock. A field. A man is really someone when he can work land."

Thinking of her husband who had fled, Claudia had her own opinion about what made a man, but she let the moment pass.

"You gathered all this livestock and herded them back here?" Claudia looked out at the paddock of animals and was genuinely impressed. "That's quite an endeavor."

"I've had my setbacks, no doubt. Couldn't have done it without the dogs." *Though sometimes in spite of the dogs*, he thought as he remembered the gutted ewes in the field.

The two stood side by side, leaning on the fence, looking out at his farm. They spoke of the people they had lost but stopped short of describing the horror they had seen.

"I'm Claudia," she said with a small bow of her head.

"Percy... Hounder." He bowed his head hoping she did not see the uncertainty in his eyes. "What did you do in the baron's household?"

Despite being drawn to him and his honesty, Claudia had too much to lose. She shrugged her shoulders and changed the subject. "What do you think of the baroness?"

"I had never spoken to her directly until today. Never was included in any festivities. A dog boy doesn't speak to a baroness but...I don't mean to be impertinent, but I heard people talk about her cruelty."

Claudia acknowledged it with a look.

Percy shook his head in disbelief. "I hear she cast a woman out the same day one of her newborn twins died. Made her pack up and off the property within the hour. Blood still warm on the sheets." He shuddered. "Frankly," he said leaning toward her and lowering his voice, "I'm glad to have never crossed her path before. She beats her dog, I hear!"

"Witnessing death will soften the heart," Claudia said, reciting the agreed-upon explanation.

Perry shrugged his shoulders.

Claudia realized that now that he was less of a threat, she was unprepared for the visit: a proper welcome to the neighborhood required some bit of food to offer, a chicken to start a brood, even just a small pot of soup. She had nothing. And she had to retract her claim that the baroness meant to run him off. "The children are recapturing the chickens," Claudia said. "I'll bring you one. I spoke in haste, earlier. The... baroness is wondering what sort of saplings you have."

"Pear. Apple."

"Very good." Claudia wanted to say that it was good to have him here. Good to have an honest man among them, one this handsome. Good that you did not bed the baroness and especially good that you are not the father of Daisy. In companionable silence, they watched the sheep grazing.

"A new mother?" he asked with a smile and a bow of his head. She looked down to see breast milk seeping through her bodice. She quickly covered her chest with her arms.

He shook his head. "No need for shame. It's nature's way."

She hurried away but would repeat his words to herself late at night as evidence of his surprisingly kind nature.

~ * ~ * ~ * ~

Later that week, MT stole away from the activity and walked undetected through a copse of trees to the secret cottage. Roiling with emotion she sat down on the fur-wrapped chair. She was unaccustomed to the regard shown to her by the staff. No, not staff, she thought, her maids. Her servants, people who waited for her command and were governed by her words. She had hungered for this position as a way to care for people, she had thought, but now that she had it she wondered how much of its allure had been because of the power that came with it. The first few days the curtsying startled her but now she sailed by the bent knees and bowed heads as if it really was her birthright. She had allowed a pride of ownership to creep into her, as if the smooth running of the household was an indication of her worth. All her life she had been taught to dampen any sign of pride, so these new feelings made her almost itchy. More than the prospect of discovery or the punishment that could be meted out to her, it was the unearned praise that made her uncomfortable.

And she had just recently discovered that there was a high price for this new position: she heard the maids giggling in the pantry but saw them clamp their lips and straighten their shoulders as she approached. Their reverie in the kitchen at night where they now ate was halted the minute she crossed the threshold. In the midst of laughter, they would say "oh, we're not talking about anything, milady," and there was nothing she could do to be included. She learned not to disturb them, to keep her distance, shun their company. Claudia was her only companion and even she was consumed by her love for little Daisy, ensconced in a family of which MT was not a part. Some nights, if Claudia was busy MT ate alone at the head table, feeling small and abandoned. The isolation was unexpected. When she was alone with her cart and bearskin on the road, her loneliness was understandable. But in her past she had been surrounded by groups of women looking the same, praying the same, standing, kneeling, and bowing heads in unison. The worst form of punishment was being separated from others. Locked in her cell or face down on the church floor while the others worked in the garden – it was the banishment that had brought the real pain. Now, her mind was happy, but her heart ached. She had traded warm companionship for the cold idea. She purchased her plan for the community with her own banishment. Frustrated but included, or expressive and alone. Those weren't the only two choices in life, were they?

She ran her hand over the soft, rabbit fur cover on the chair, and moved to the bed. She took off the mirrored cap and ran her hands through hair that had been a substance only seen as it fell from the razor's edge to the floor. The clothing she had been wearing since coming to the manor was made of beautiful cloth, but this bed cover was something different. This cottage, this luxury, was sensual, and she supposed it was sexual. More foreign than stature and power, it made her nervous in a different way.

She looked around to the far corners of the cottage to be sure all the shutters were closed, that the only light was coming in from stained glass windows high above a man's head. She looped her thumbs into the lacing at the side of her dress, hesitated, then closed her eyes and loosened her dress, letting it fall to the floor. In a rush she pulled her slip over her head and lay down naked on the rabbit fur cover. She had spent eight months under the bearskin pelt and its thick, uneven fur had been comforting amid the horror, but this fur was...heavenly. This was sinful.

Hadn't she taken a vow of poverty? Now she wore fine kidskin gloves and a heavy cloak against the morning chill when she walked out to the kitchen garden. The maid was pulling weeds in nothing but a thin shawl, her hands red and chapped from the cold. MT fought with herself to keep from wrapping the girl in the cloak and pulling off her own gloves, but Claudia had made it clear that too much generosity was suspicious. What would happen if she lived in this much luxury, this kind of indulgence, she wondered, as she wrapped her naked body in the rabbit fur cover, sighed deeply over the baffling, delicious feeling on her skin, and fell asleep.

She returned to the manor before sunset more aware of her skin than at any time in her life. That evening, a maid knocked on the library door and entered at her command. With a frightened look on her face, she beckoned MT who immediately got down from her perch to see what new danger they were facing. The maid walked down the hall a few feet in front of her and then opened the door to a room, quickly closing it behind them with a smile. MT was confused. The room was golden with candlelight and held a large steaming bathtub. The women flanked each side of a path to the bathtub, each holding a basket of flower petals. The ones closest to the tub gently poured the flowers into the steaming water and Claudia, who had been standing behind the door, took MT by the hand.

"We are all so grateful to you, milady." Claudia stepped behind MT and started untying the cords that held her dress together.

"No, no," said MT with surprise and spun around while clutching her dress. She could not possibly disrobe in front of these women, in front of anyone at all. A second woman dropped to her knees and took off MT's slippers, then her socks and only the smile on Claudia's face kept her from lashing out and running away.

"Thank you, Baroness," each woman said as they removed

her sleeves, her stockings, and then, in her linen shift, they guided MT to steps that were on the outside and the inside of the tub. An upholstered bench for her to lie on would keep her head above water, another accommodation built for the little baroness. They gently removed the cap on her head.

"Your hair is so lustrous."

With soft, soapy cloths they washed her arms, though she crossed them over her breasts when they were done.

She kept looking at Claudia to see if this was a prank, and she tensed, waiting for biting derision, but everywhere she looked all she saw were women thanking her for rescuing them. The linen slip clung to her, but no one pointed and laughed.

"It's alright," Claudia kept saying to her as they floated more petals on the water and stroked her hair, her cheeks, touched her in ways that she had never experienced. Were they being attentive only to gossip about her in the kitchen? Even as a small girl in the nunnery bathing was frightening as her nakedness exposed her to even more ridicule, and it seemed that no lock on any door was strong enough to keep the nuns out and stop their mischief. She had nearly died as a young child, so short that she could climb the stairs into the tub but could not haul herself out again and it seemed that no one heard her cries as she clung to the rim. Thankfully, hot water was in such demand that a novice outside the door, not yet hardened with cruelty, broke the latch and helped her out. Yet today she was surrounded by kindness that seemed genuine. She kept looking at Claudia who smiled and nodded, signaling that she should allow these ministrations as part of a baroness's due. Whether it was the reaction of a baroness or not, MT could not stop herself from sobbing into her hands while they scrubbed her back. Here was another kind of vulnerability and fear. They held a sheet up to shield her when she stepped out and wrapped her in the softest towel she had ever touched and she continued to cry as they sat her down and cleaned her nails, brushed her hair. They had found the lady's oils and creams deep inside the closet in this room and they kneaded it into her skin, all of them smiling and gentle. "We are so grateful milady." Helping her into a brocade robe brought by Claudia from the library closet, each of them curtsied before taking their basket or cloth and leaving the room. Finally, Claudia and MT stood alone.

"How could you do that to me? Let them laugh over the way I look!"

Claudia was stunned. "The way you look just saved 30 people's lives."

"You know what I mean," she said tearfully.

Claudia shook her head in disappointment. "Well, I invite you to consider...that you are cherished just the way you are."

CHAPTER EIGHT

A week after Claudia had delivered two chickens to the farm, Percy's dogs were barking with urgency at the chicken coop, and Percy was surprised to find not a fox but a man outside holding a single egg, with a bee-hive shaped oven on a cart between him and the dogs.

Merek, the baker, could think of no excuse for his theft.

"A single egg, sir," he said. "I am unaccustomed to farms that are working. It seems the countryside is all food for the taking. I beg forgiveness."

Percy called off the dogs and they trotted to flank him, still alert, while Percy silently assessed the man in front of him.

Merek decided to bargain. "Perhaps I could work for you, in return for food," Merek said, though having spent a lifetime at a bread oven he knew nothing of sheep or chickens.

Percy saw that Merek had only one hand. "As you say, it's a single egg."

"I can swing an axe." Merek pointed to it strapped to the side of his wagon.

"You're a baker?"

"I have an oven, don't I?" Merek hoped that was proof enough, as he placed his palm flat on the cold pottery shell in front of him.

"You should check with the lady of the manor," Percy said. "I think they're in need of a baker."

Merek said nothing, but was certain that if they needed a baker, they didn't need him.

Merek had always been an early riser, but he had taken to the road because the ground was stony under his bedroll, and he had a sinking feeling of hopelessness that threatened to keep him wrapped up and immobile all day. In speaking to the woman with the baby and narrowly escaping capture by the sheriff, he was exaggerating only a bit when he told her there was a lack of grain and lack of customers. He had never really been a baker. Not in the true sense of it. And in the weeks since he saw her, things had gotten worse. In his fear of contagion, he had walked so far east that grains were hardly grown and there was no one left to harvest them nor working millstones to grind them.

When he reached this manor, he had stood immobilized in the middle of the road, looking at the silent mill on the river, the chapel to his right, the chaotic farm ahead, and the road that led uphill to a manor house. Could he throw himself on the mercy of the gentry inside? He had a small packet of rosemary; a bag of elderflower that needed to be dried before it molded. The berries he had collected had already been spoiled for lack of flour to embed them in and honestly, he wouldn't know what to do if there had been. An egg for strength before he approached the manor was all he had wanted.

Despite his possession of the only oven for miles around, Merek thought of himself as more of a fire tender than an actual baker. Women brought their bread already risen, already filled with herbs and butter, made of flour ground elsewhere. He was popular because he was a storyteller, someone who brought news and gossip from other villages and he had a flair for the dramatic which charmed the women as their loaves baked and he tended the fire.

He didn't remember the accident that took his hand, just the feeling of being jostled in his father's arms as he ran in a panic while reciting prayers, toward an overgrown thatched hut. "Thank God for the witch," his father would say throughout Merek's life, and more than once he had heard his father including her in his dinner table prayers, though under his breath so Merek's mother wouldn't hear.

The hand was lost just above the wrist and his recouperation was a hazy collage of bones, stones and herbs hanging above him, his father on his knees by the bed gripping Merek's ankle as if to keep him from floating away.

They may have been in the hut for a week or a month, but he remembered his mother's fury when they returned, her accusations of infidelity, an exhaustive list of the work she had shouldered without his father, and then her biting assessment of Merek, an inspection head to toe as if he was a lamb too thin to butcher. She lifted his arm and regarded the bandage tied to the healing stub, and without a word, dropped it and walked back to her mixing bowl.

His father tended to Merek's injury every day, but they sat on a low wall behind the bakehouse, out of earshot of his mother, and his father was chipper over Merek's progress in healing, extolled his bravery and reassured him that his future would be barely marred for lack of a hand. When he healed, Merek carried armloads of wood from the forest and his father taught him to swing an axe one-handed.

But Merek had no idea how to bake and his ignorance was surprising. Parents taught their children the skills of their family; the seamstress taught her children a clean stitch; the blacksmith had his children hammer the red-hot metal in rhythm. Unlike them, though, Merek's mother had jealously guarded her recipes, never let him measure ingredients and didn't teach him how to know when the dough was risen but not over-proofed. She kept her husband ignorant as well, as if even those who loved her might steal what was hers. Merek and his father built the fire, raked it down to coals and then turned the oven over to his mother. She waved them away when she was working, wouldn't let either of them look over her shoulder. It created resentment like a sailor's knot in Merek's chest. A man chops wood, his father used to tell him, making excuses for their exclusion, and he protected his son from his mother's disdain. He also smoothed the rough edges of her conversations with patrons whenever they were stung by one of her frequent, sour and mean-spirited comments.

His miserly mother, stingy with affection and love, was

generous with butter and honey, though, and treated her baked goods and bread with tenderness, cooing at them as if they were kittens, proud of them like she should be of her son. She produced perfect bread, baps, and rolls with crunchy crusts and tender insides. Her honey cakes and fruit torts were carried on large trays, arranged in perfectly even and identical rows to the manor house of a now-distant village and the lady of the manor often took his mother's baked goods as gifts for others.

Just once, Merek had thought, he wanted to bake something that lit up a woman's face. Something sublime. And especially to prove his mother wrong, to wrest from her the jewels she wouldn't share.

His mother was as proud of the bakehouse as she was of her work (though the building belonged to a noble). Not a fire-hazard of a wooden hut, not a tiny cottage with grass growing from the thatch, their bakehouse was built of stone with tall, straight walls and a peaked roof almost taller than the village church. Its roof had been created with overlapping slate shingles laid in a fish-scale pattern, elegant and exact. A low wall defined a small courtyard behind the bakehouse where Merek sat with his father, and unknown to his mother, this became Merek's domain when he was no older than 12. In the spring and summer, sometimes even in drizzling rain when his father sat inside, women would sit beside him on the wall outside and whisper their troubles, their desires, their hopes for harvest or children, their confusion over harsh husbands. Perhaps because he had been injured they thought he understood pain and since he wasn't a priest he would not be shocked or judgmental. In contrast, the stories and reports they gave inside the bakehouse while sitting on a bench with the other women waiting for their loaves were glowing and prideful reports, so Merek became the keeper of secret fears and longings. When he was older and went into the forest for wood without his father the woodcutters used him as well. They would lean on their axe, out of sight behind a tree, and confide in him about money troubles, temptations, and failing strength. To them, a man missing a hand was less than a man and so in no position to judge. Or perhaps it was that listening to the sorrows of others had made Merek so kind that it showed on his face.

When he was old enough to demand that he be elevated from a woodcutter to a baker he had a confrontation with his mother that was clumsy and unsuccessful. He went to bed bitter and frustrated. The next day a tremendous cold front descended on them, harsher than anyone remembered. Despite his father's protests, though, his parents had gone to the bishop's mill to fetch flour and as the sun started to set, a snowstorm pounded the village. Merek had paced the floor, fuming over his mother's refusal to teach him and yet worried for their safety. Suddenly, the family's horse burst into the bakehouse for the first time in its docile life. It shook its mane, sending snow to the floor and when it shook a second time needles of ice broke off its mane and pelted Merek. He had never known an animal to be so desperate for warmth that it would break into the bakehouse, though on many winter evenings he had found the horse and the neighbor's sheep clustered against the outside back wall nearest the oven. He rubbed it down, dried it, stoked the fire and spoke to it softly to calm them both. If the horse had returned, why had his parents not ridden the horse home?

In the morning, a stableman arrived to show him.

Merek followed the stableman through snow that came up to his thighs, but he ran awkwardly when he saw the family's cart parked against the high fence of the abbey. There was two feet of snow on top of the flour bags and earlier that morning, the stableman had scraped snow off with his gloved hand to see if the flour, now frozen into huge blocks, was ruined. As he absently scraped at the snow with his mind on the buttery glory of bread, he jumped back in surprise. He had uncovered a woman's hand, frozen with its grip on a flour sack. He hauled himself into the cart, pried several frozen flour bags loose and hurled them into the snowbank. The baker was frozen while curled with a flour bag in her arms, her leg over the sack like it was her lover, with a sack behind her as a buffer against her husband, whose arm was stretched out to protect her. They must have pulled the sacks over the top of themselves in the hopes of keeping out the cold.

Merek gripped the edge of the wagon fighting alternating waves of sorrow and rage. His tightfisted mother had refused to leave her flour for fear of theft, and his father had turned the horse loose to give it a chance to live, then lay down beside his wife with a devotion that Merek didn't think she deserved. Even on their deathbed, the baker kept her husband at bay with a sack between them, when their body warmth might have saved them. Probably not, but still, her last act was a refusal, and it hurt Merek to see it.

There could be no burials in that weather, and no chance of

straightening the corpses since stiffness would set in before the bodies thawed. He knew they would go into the ground curled up like babies, and there was no telling when that would be. "We'll move them into the milk-house, lad," the stableman said quietly, "since we brought the milk indoors a week ago when the weather first turned. That will protect them against the wolves," he said, "if any venture out in this cold." His voice trailed off in sympathy.

If Merek had been trained, he would have been old enough to take over the bakehouse, even though he had only one hand, but as it was, he would be unmasked as untrained. Merek chose not to reveal his ignorance, first claiming that grief closed the bakery and when the thaw came and he said prayers over his parent's graves, he brought out the mobile oven from a back building and mumbled excuses to the villagers about wanting to see the world, ready to bring baked goods to the earth's far corners. Instead, he cut and hauled wood, walking from hamlet to village, one handle of the cart customized so he could push it with his foreshortened arm. He worked the circuit of fairs and farmer's markets, shepherding the women's dough balls in and out of the oven and telling stories. And because they thought they'd never see him again, his customers first told him their best stories, then their darkest secrets. It was a decent living, until it wasn't.

Facing Percy that morning, though, he threw his shoulders back to make him appear stronger. "Let me stock your woodpile in return for a meal and a bed, sir. I'm strong enough to be put to any task."

"Do you know anything about sheep?"

"Nothing," Merek said.

"Well, attend to the woodpile and lay a fire as the day ends, if you would sir. The manor has no flour and no wheat to harvest that I know of but there's no other baker there."

The following morning at the manor house, the gates were open to Merek immediately because his oven was such a welcome sight, and he was asked to stand in the middle of the courtyard while the young boy ran jubilantly for the mistress. Merek's arrival brightened the mood of everyone who saw him, though he explained that he was just a lowly woodcutter.

He banished thoughts of himself, though, when he saw the lady of the manor striding toward him. She was the most oddly shaped woman he had ever seen, like an egg, wider and shorter than anyone he had ever met, no taller than a child.

"I understand you are a baker," MT said to him with a grin. "Is this your first visit to… my manor?"

"Indeed, milady. I have ventured so far east that there is no grain to work with and I am reduced to…"

"You are welcome here. Our oven sits idle for want of flour, and we have few men to chop wood. We are a small community… I mean, my household is small as of yet, but we open our doors to you."

Claudia, her baby on her hip, had seen the oven cart from the second floor and came out to greet him. "Merek!"

He brightened. "So good to see you free!" he said, though he chose not to ask her how it had happened. "And how is little Daisy?"

She smiled broadly: he recognized the child as hers and she turned to MT. "His bread melts in the mouth, milady."

Merek smiled weakly. It was the bread of the last woman who had stopped at his oven, a rare occurrence in a depopulated world.

MT stood back and put her hands on her broad hips. "Then we shall endeavor to find you supplies." She turned to Claudia. "Take him to the kitchen and have him fed. Baker, there is no doubt that the cook will make clear to you who is in charge there but when you are sated, have one of the girls take you to the bakery and then give us your estimation of what must be done to make it right. Claudia will help you settle in."

Conferring in the library that night, Claudia paced the floor.

"Settle in? Are we settling in now? What have I said about that?"

"I know. But perhaps they can stay when you and I decide we have to go," MT said. More than anything, MT wanted to stay. To continue to build her clan.

Claudia noted that MT was now speaking of them as a pair and though she was touched by the companionship, she wondered if that made her complicit in the pending theft of the gold.

MT was sitting on a small stool, trying to beckon the wolfhound to her. Despite its earlier obedience, the wolfhound continued to sniff any part of her that was exposed, and when she raised her hand to pet it, it shied away in expectation of the baroness's cruelty. Claudia put an end to her efforts.

"The baroness was notoriously cruel to the dog. It doesn't help you to change that."

"I will not abuse an animal for any reason," MT said.

"You cannot fool a dog. If you win over this dog you are exposed as someone who is not the baroness."

The women glared at each other, at an impasse.

"More important is the situation with our people," MT said, rising from the stool with a sigh. "We leave them to the Crown's mercy if we run away. Somehow, we all have to go."

Claudia wondered why she hadn't already fled with Daisy. She was free now and it would make sense to get Daisy as far away from this place as possible. But where would she go? She didn't want to go to the city. "Perhaps you could take the veil again."

"Never."

"Maybe we have gone on a pilgrimage," Claudia said, jostling little Daisy to help her sleep.

MT warmed to the subject. "The Crusade. The baroness and her entire household joined the siege of Jerusalem. No, that's absurd. But it has to be everyone. We can't leave the women here to be scooped up by the bishop again and the men to be indentured to the earl."

Claudia thought of the enormity of the task but nodded. "Truly, we must have an escape plan. Someone is bound to arrive who knows the truth."

The next evening, someone did.

~ * ~ * ~ * ~

Unfortunately, the procurements of Simon in the surrounding villages drew the attention of a dower old marchioness who announced her intention to visit the manor by sending a tersely delivered pronouncement with a page who arrived just hours before the marchioness.

Both Claudia and MT rushed into the library and locked the door.

"That's it," Claudia said. "Unmasked. Then executed. We should hide. Or flee."

They heard the alarm bell, announcing the marchioness's arrival.

"She has already been told that I'm here," MT said. "We have to make this convincing. Perhaps one last time."

Claudia pulled out a black dress with exasperation and shook it at her. "You're in mourning, after all," she reminded MT. "For your husband, the baron."

"Yes, of course, for my husband, whose name is…"

"Cedric."

"Right. Cedric. My beloved Cedric."

"I wouldn't go that far. They were cruel to the staff and cold to each other."

Claudia helped her struggle into the dress, both anxious as they heard the marchioness's cane on the floor. Claudia chuckled as MT put her arms through the wrong holes and didn't know how to lace the bodice before the skirt went on. A nun's habit was a simple shift with a slip beneath if she was lucky. When Claudia stood back to marvel at the exact fit, MT looked down and put a hand to her chest.

"There's a piece missing! Surely there's something to

cover…" She was horrified. Her breasts were inches from exposure. "I can't go out like this!"

Claudia smiled indulgently. She stepped to the closet and pulled a piece of black lace from a peg and wrapped it around MT's neck but when she slipped it into the dress near her breasts MT jerked back and finished the task herself.

Claudia shook her head. "Amazing that it fits. Down to the exact length of the sleeves. The tailoring on the hips. Are you sure you're not a bastard twin?"

"I don't know who my father was. Perhaps the father of the baroness, passing through our hamlet…"

"No time for that," Claudia stopped her. "Focus on the marchioness." Claudia quickly rattled off anything she had heard around the manor: the old woman's lineage; the previous deaths of all her children except one; and marriage of her brother; the extent of her land; the last time she was at the manor which according to gossip was two Christmases before the Great Mortality when she had gotten drunk and fallen asleep at the high table.

But MT was focused on the previous conversation. What if she was related to the baroness? A bastard, but still related and so…entitled? The thought didn't sit well with her. And she could never prove it. It would make her Daisy's aunt, though. No. No sense pursuing this, she thought. She shoved the black cap onto her head and stuffed her hair in just as a maid knocked on the door.

MT considered how to continue the deception. "Remove all the platforms and stairs," she told the maid. "Especially at the high table. Prepare…something to eat. Rabbit, no doubt."

MT strode down the hall toward the old marchioness who was hunched over her cane like a woman who hadn't fully stood in a decade. She was dressed for a fete though dust had collected in the folds of her skirt. MT wanted to guide the old woman to a chair and have her feet warmed but stood imperiously and let the dowager shuffle toward her before MT curtsied. They had made slow progress toward making the manor house worthy of a marchioness's visit. The windows and walls were still bare, the breakfronts and cupboard doors crooked but closed. They had quality place settings for only half of a banquet and the cloth for the high table had just been finished the day before.

The elkhound walked down the hall, pressing its side against the wall. MT, without looking at it, clicked her fingers for it and when it came to her side she tried to run her palm from the dog's head to the place on its back where the baroness in the portrait rested her hand. The dog flinched and moved away. The dowager stopped as it bolted and shook her head disapprovingly.

"I'll never understand why you let it in the house," she said. "What do you call it, again?"

MT was silent. What was the cruelest thing you could do to a dog? "A name?" MT scoffed. "I have my limits."

The marchioness cackled but as she drew near to steady herself on MT's shoulder, she shuddered at the vision in the black cap. The marchioness had offered to visit the baroness because the woman's reappearance was putting a kink in the plans of the earl, her son-in-law, and as she was not one to sit idly by like her daughter, the marchioness had her coach readied. Besides, she was desperate to be among people of quality and it wasn't until she arrived that she remembered the loathsome quality of the baroness and the way all squirmed in the tiny woman's company.

"Where have you been this year?" the marchioness said as they shuffled slowly toward the Great Room and high table.

"Eight months," MT corrected her, remembering Claudia's timeline. She sighed deeply. "Sequestered and grieving for the baron in a northern abbey." She knew of a distant one, isolated and unlikely to have been visited by the marchioness or anyone who knew her. "Even when boiled the water smells like horse hooves and there's a rank odor coming off the walls." MT knew that was true because during one of her visits she discovered that they polished the wood with rancid fat. The marchioness sputtered her surprise.

MT continued. "The only thing worse than the petty rules was the quality of the food."

"I cannot imagine." The marchioness shook her head.

"Up and down on one's knees at all hours of the night. Idiocy passing for divine inspiration." The scorn poured out of her, a relief to not suppress it, to not bow one's head and take it. "Meat the color of morning fog. Vile things swimming in a bloody broth. It will give me nightmares if the great dying doesn't."

They ate grilled rabbit while the fire crackled behind them. The marchioness shredded the rabbit into tiny pieces with her fingers and made noises as she chewed. MT thought of the wax needed to treat the wainscoting on the far wall.

Because the platform had been hastily removed and the

chairs placed side by side, closely together, the dowager could only see the top of MT's head. The cap reflected her own death, the nasty bits of her that would be worked on by worms but as she turned away from it, the marchioness was suddenly filled with gratitude for the sickness's sparing of her daughter and son-in-law, and for her own survival. It was a warmth to which she was not accustomed. What a remarkable gift from so horrid a woman.

Even before the Great Mortality, the marchioness had avoided this manor house and its gloomy residents, but was now secretly, smugly pleased to have heard that the entire estate had been ransacked. Using the baron's land for a jail was an excellent idea, a final indignity that put these sour members of the gentry in their place. She had hoped that some of the booty would have wound up on her own shelves, especially as her foolish son-in-law was struggling with their new condition of being rich in unworked land. While her family had fled north, the sickness had wiped out almost all of his serfs and the rest had run away. There were no rents to collect, no crops to sell.

His plan of rounding up the peasantry showed initiative, she thought, and demonstrated that he was a man who knew his own power. He mistakenly believed, however, that she was unaware of the roundup, the sheriff and the jail, but she had a much better network of informants than he realized. At the same time, both of them would keep the knowledge from her daughter, who would be ashamed that they had to go to such lengths. Now that this dreadful baroness had returned and kept the first batch of peasants for herself, they were behind schedule in their planting and powerless to gather their wayward livestock.

"The baron…" MT began, then shook her head. "I have seen so much death. It humbles and softens the heart. But let's not dwell on it. It's too awful to relive."

"Quite right," the old woman said but ate quickly and announced her departure. The flinching dog, the horrid hat. Some things never change, the marchioness concluded as she struggled down the hall faster than when she arrived. The maids seemed less cowed and miserable, though. She thought she had heard laughter from the kitchen.

The marchioness stood at the door of her carriage surveying the courtyard where a maid carried a basket of wild sorrel.

"Girl! What have you to eat here?"

"Rabbit, your grace. More rabbit than anyone can stand."

The marchioness waved her off and when she was out of earshot, crooked her finger to a tall footman holding the door to her carriage. He bent to hear her low voice.

"Gather two of your best," she said quietly, "and then see me about a plan."

Where there were rabbits, she knew, there were valuable fur pelts. For the taking. No need to tell the others and the sheriff was busy staffing the earl's manor. She would use her own men and keep knowledge of her larcenous plan–and the money it produced – to herself.

CHAPTER NINE

Jacob explained to his favorite rabbits that a great joy had come over their land. She had returned.

He had waited for eight long months. He had stood on the warren lodge parapet with Petunia the Bunny and Julia the Flop-Eared in his arms as they watched the first flight of everyone from the manor, including those adults he had grown to regard as his parents, then had watched as stealthy and ragged people had broken into the house and made off with the goods; lastly, the small band of men beating themselves bloody as they trudged down the street. From the roof lookout on the other side, Petunia (festooned with a bow), Julia (sporting a fine necklace of wooden beads) and Jacob had watched as sheep outside of their pens wandered across the dale, chickens outside of coops proliferate in the bushes, Mother Nature rushing into death's void.

"Now, people have returned," he explained, nuzzling Petunia's ear. "Healthy people who need the rabbits' warmth and the flesh of your cousins to be well in the world and there is nothing more important than being of service to others."

He put Petunia and Julia under his bed, the words pouring out of him now that he was back from a day of trapping the bucks and dropping them into individual cages. If left to roam free, they would kill the newborn rabbits so they could mate with the does again, and that would not do. Not now that the manor house was in need of stew.

"The house in need of stew," he chanted to himself, "the house in need of stew."

Later in the week, Jacob arrived with his arms laden with rabbit pelts that he presented to MT with a ceremonious bow.

"They are beautiful, Jacob," she said, running her hand along the brown and white pelt and thinking of the bedcover on her naked skin. "Evidence of your skill and care."

He met her eyes then looked down again at the floor. "Will you visit me, milady?"

"Excellent idea, Jacob. I will." She should see this rabbit warren, as it was clearly a contributor to the manor's wealth, and it would do to visit him, as he had been alone so long, she had heard.

Later that afternoon, MT started up the hill with a parcel of vegetables from the garden and two filets of grilled fish as gifts for Jacob. Even a baroness would not arrive empty-handed, MT hoped. It had been difficult to convince Claudia to let her go alone and MT wasn't sure why she was so excited to go.

Like every warren lodge she had seen, it was a solid building of thick stone walls with slit windows on both floors and a single small door on the ground floor which made it a miniature fortress against armed marauders intent on the valuable pelts.

From the parapet of the warren lodge, Jacob waved down to MT, spoke to the rabbit in his arms and made it wave to her as well. MT marveled at what he must have seen these years from that spot.

Jacob had washed and was in clean clothing. Even his woolen cap looked clean. He bowed to MT when she came in. The rabbit he cradled was in a gauzy dress with a white bone necklace and MT touched the flounce and smiled. He bowed to her when he showed her the trapping tools, bowed when he presented the gutting table and bowed before he showed her the stretching rack. Finally, she seized his arm.

"Enough bowing, Jacob," she said softly.

They climbed the stairs to his living quarters, and he pulled a stool from under the table. It was exactly the height for her short legs and extra wide, as if it had been made for her, and she settled in. A pile of scrap fabric and a small box of wooden beads sat on the floor. Jacob sat down cross-legged and with a huge grin, handed her the box of beads and a bit of leather thong, as if she would know what to do. He pulled a needle from a flap on his vest and went back to work as if she wasn't sitting there, baffled. He was making new dresses for the rabbits, he explained, though he might make vests for the bucks who had recently felt slighted by the does' finery. The dresses were gossamer, with lace and beading, evidence of hours of work and finer fabric than peasant clothing. As he sewed, he spun out stories of feuds and friendships of the pillow mound queens, and MT relaxed into his happy world of make-believe while she strung beads in patterns of her own design, some for their necks, some for their ears.

"Oh no!" Jacob exclaimed. "Not blue beads for Petunia! Red and yellow only, milady."

"Ah, I beg her pardon," she said, smiling into his green eyes. A delightful boy in a man's body.

Tentatively, she invented characters with fabric scraps and made them converse. He told her of the rabbit's response. They sewed skirts and little kerchiefs for the rabbits. Hours went by. No subterfuge, no stress, just silliness. The stuff of life that had drawn her to the bear trainer's world. If she had ever played like this as a toddler, she couldn't remember it, and after being sent to the nunnery there was no play, no frivolity, the little girls as stern and lifeless as the oldest nun. She rubbed her face against Petunia's silky rabbit fur.

At noon they ate the fish and carrots, and when MT wiped her mouth with her hand she sprung up from the stool. "Show me these queendoms," she ordered happily.

He stood and smiled. "The coneygarths of the queens!"

He kept his hand on her shoulder as they walked carefree to the first colony where he traced in the air the labyrinth of tunnels underneath. The air was crisp and fragrant with apple blossoms. Three-foot ditches with water the rabbits wouldn't cross outlined each pillow mound and he asked the rabbit queen's permission to cross it. With a flourish he introduced MT to the rabbits who emerged. She watched the rabbits huddle together, their noses twitching. At the next coneygarth, this one of Eleanor, he helped her lie across the mound, which perplexed and excited her, then sprinkled her with carrot tops and set a rabbit on her belly to munch them. She laughed until the rabbit bounced off.

MT took his arm as they returned to the part of the warren nearest the lodge. He showed her the woven birthing cages where the does were safe from the bucks, showed her the varied hay he grew for their food, pointed out the pillow mounds in the distance where they had been, and she saw the pegs that flew ribbons in different colors—the ribbons that had first drawn her to the manor. MT looked down at her dress and thought she recognized one of them.

"Such festive ribbons," she said.

"Given by you, my dear Baroness," Jacob said, dropping to one knee and kissing her hand. "A ribbon for each time you rode me."

MT raised her eyebrows, considering what he had said. Rode him? Mounted and rode him? He was certainly handsome enough: the maids lit up at the sight of him. And old enough. But the baroness's liaison? Her mouth open, she looked out at the dozens of ribbons. Dozens of rides. "In the cottage," she said quietly.

"The secret cottage," Jacob whispered.

MT sighed, heat rising in her chest, and she gently slipped the woolen cap from his head. A mass of silky golden hair fell to his shoulders, and she closed her eyes briefly, then ran her hand down its length, stroked his cheek, lifted his chin with her hand. Jacob had been the baroness's lover. Jacob was Daisy's father. He didn't notice that she wasn't the actual baroness. And since he didn't shy away from her like the baroness's poor dog, perhaps Jacob was the one person with whom the baroness could be kind, the only one who received her tenderness and gave it to her in return. Maybe the baroness's time with him was the only time she could play. MT could only hope so.

She smiled down at him, but the alarm bell sounded from the far wall of the manor house. She jumped, dropped her hand, kissed the crown of his head and quickly headed back to the manor, leaving him on his knee at Queen Phillipa's mound.

The joy and freedom of the morning dissipated as MT ran. She was so exasperated by the now-familiar sound of the sheriff's posse and its damnable wagon of misfortunes arriving in the lower barn that when she arrived there she didn't have to pretend to be an enraged and embittered woman.

The sheriff shifted on his feet. "These men are for the earl. He's due at the end of the week to fetch them."

"And he expects me to feed them in the meantime!"

Baudwin shrugged. "I'll station…"

"You'll do no such thing. I'll have my own men guard them," she said though she knew she had only the old man, the orphan child and the one-handed Merek. Simon was off on another supply run. She looked into the corrals. This group seemed comprised of the especially young or the sadly weak. "Though it seems a milkmaid could knock them down." Some had split lips and bruised faces. "Do you have to beat them before you bring them?"

Baudwin seemed surprised by her concern.

"So that I have to patch them up as well as feed them," she said, recovering from her display of compassion.

"The earl. End of the week, milady," Baudwin said, bowing and motioning the men he had delegated as guards to return to their horses. Mounting his own, he wondered which was crueler: the earl's campaign to capture them or the baroness's jail.

The arrival of the prisoners put MT in a foul mood, and she decided that another chance to play with Jacob and the rabbits would restore her day. She dug in the baroness's closet for scraps and when she found none, she took a knife from the desk and cut little bits of lace from the woman's underskirt, a length of brocade from a hem, a fine woven pattern of pears and doves from two sleeves. She hid them in a plain cloth and climbed the hill, happier with each step and when she announced herself and climbed the stairs to his rooms, he was ebullient as well.

"For Petunia," she said. "I can't stay but…"

He took her hand and led her to the spot between the bed and the wall and they fell into their carefree chatter about queens, coneys, and their dresses.

MT returned before sundown, hopefully without being missed, but as she reached the library she was intercepted by Claudia who curtsied quickly and put her hands on her hips.

"You left a stack of pelts on the sideboard here, milady," she said with feigned timidity because of the servants in the hall. She gestured to the empty spot. "Stolen. And two of the kitchen maids are gone as well." Claudia motioned for them to go into the library, where she paced the floor with anger as MT climbed to the desk.

"A noble would know to guard those pelts!"

"This is confusing, being the lady of the manor and yet…not." MT sighed with resignation. "I suppose they are the most valuable thing in the building."

"No. You are mistaken." Claudia charged toward her. "The most valuable thing here is your identity, and now," she lowered her voice and looked again to be sure the library door was closed. "Now the entire staff, including two who have fled out into the world, may not know your secret, but have evidence of your un-gentry-like behavior. Our lives, MT, our lives hang in the balance."

MT sighed deeply and shook her head. She was still furious over the prisoners, resentful that a pall had fallen over her day of fun with Jacob, and now insulted by the maids' disloyalty. She strode into the kitchen and announced that any pelts would now to be counted twice a day and locked in the baroness's library.

"And take the elkhound to the farm with the other dogs," she said sharply to Claudia, who saw that her words might be stinging but the move was for the good of the dog.

MT slept fitfully, seeing Jacob's golden hair and her hand caressing his cheek, waking up puzzled by the pressure in her chest. The baroness had broken her bonds of marriage, committed adultery, bore an illegitimate child: there was no reason to long for the woman's position. Furthermore, MT now possessed knowledge that would be important to her friend: it might put Claudia's mind at ease to learn that Daisy's father was a man incapable of demanding the child and who may not even know the child was partly his. Or it might be news that would disturb Claudia further, knowing that Daisy could be taken away and raised by a father who was not really an adult, or even that the child might grow up to be simple-minded herself. Knowing the anxiety that Claudia lived with, MT should wake her immediately with the news, but she held still and tried to sleep, suddenly more protective of Jacob than Claudia.

It may have been that MT was thinking about Jacob and attuned to his welfare that allowed her to hear the sound of the disturbance, first of Percy's dogs barking down the road, then the sound of a noisy group of men battering the doors of the warren.

MT, in her nightdress, pulled on boots, ran down the hall rousing the household. She went into the kitchen for a cleaver, but Gertrude the cook was already armed with it and guarding the pantry where the youngest women and children were huddled. The heartiest young women were crossing the courtyard with pitchforks and blades. MT ran up the hill after them though she fell behind on her short legs. She saw Percy running toward the warren with his fighting dogs.

Halfway up the hill, though, she hit upon a plan. She pulled aside two of the strongest maids. "Go to the barn," she whispered to them, "throw off the crossbar and free the prisoners. Tell them that the thieves are forcing you to set them free. If anyone asks, it was the thieves. Do you understand? And take my knife, in case."

They nodded and set out.

MT continued up the hill, frantic and afraid for Jacob. Three feet from the lodge wall, she found Petunia in her gossamer dress, dead in the grass. She panicked as she rounded the wall. Just inside the broken door, Jacob lay on the floor staring forlornly at the ceiling, blood staining the front of his nightshirt and the edge of his cap. She pushed the others aside and fell to her knees beside him. She inspected the head wound, most likely from a stone, she decided, and recited his name, gripped his hand.

All the pelts were gone, and the racks that held the skins to dry were broken and empty. The maids picked up the pieces with resignation. They had assumed that the money for their bedding and cutlery came from the sale of the pelts and now there were none. MT heard Percy's dogs snarling down the hill, men shouting, then silence.

She looked around for a bandage and tried to ignore the surprised looks of the maids who had never seen a royal tend to a lowly warrener. "Your kerchief," she snapped at a maid, and pressed it to his temple.

"Baroness, milady," he said weakly.

"I'm here Jacob. I'm here."

The maids looked askance at each other.

"Make a pallet out of something," she ordered, and was exasperated when they looked around with no idea of what to do. Julia was nowhere to be seen. Claudia arrived out of breath.

"Thank goodness you're here," MT said. "We need to get him back to the manor." Claudia took charge, and the maids made a hammock with Jacob's blanket. They started down the hill with mincing steps, struggling with the weight of him. MT stepped away and scooped up the rabbit in the dress, laid it tenderly against his chest.

"Petunia," he said, and began to cry.

They installed Jacob in an empty bedroom near the library and MT sat on a stool at his side.

"Let's have Petunia...sleep here...beside you," she said as she gingerly extracted the rabbit from his hands and laid it on the floor. She cleaned his wound and spooned broth into his mouth, and when he slept she held his hands. Claudia hovered nearby, breaking up clusters of maids who whispered about the oddity of a baroness and a bunny man.

Percy returned to the farm and as the household drifted back to bed Claudia stood in front of Jacob's door to prevent anyone from seeing MT at his side. Just as she was about to say goodnight and leave the two of them, MT removed Jacob's cap to bathe his forehead again. A tumble of hair fell on the pillow. It was blonde.

Claudia seized MT's shoulder. Could it be that Daisy's father was not a demanding royal or someone with power, but just a simple-minded warrener who made dresses for rabbits? If so, he would not challenge her parenting claim, would he? But was there a chance that Daisy would grow up to be simple-minded as well? She didn't care. Either way, Daisy was her daughter.

MT looked up at Claudia and nodded at the unspoken question.

"How long have you known?" Claudia challenged her,

since MT knew how the uncertainty ate at her. Why would she withhold such important news? "How could you keep me in the dark?"

"I'm sorry Claudia." What could she say? "He won't hurt you. I'm sure of it."

Claudia closed the door. "Does he...know?"

"No. I don't think he has any idea," MT whispered. And she would not tell him. Though it seemed selfish to keep it from him, MT couldn't risk that he would cling to Claudia. "And he...believes me to be his baroness."

Claudia sat on a chair and dropped her head into her hands, incredulous that the warrener couldn't tell the difference between the women, but then thanking the heavens that Daisy's father was not a royal. With every passing day, though, the list of potential enemies grew longer.

"We have Simon, the sheriff, the bishop and soon the earl set against us. Plus the marchioness, Percy and every member of the household with their suspicions. Jacob should know but perhaps doesn't. You actually instructed the maids to defy the sheriff and free the earl's workers!"

MT turned back to Jacob and ran her hand over his forehead. "I will not give this place up," she said, "At the very least, I will not leave them here."

Claudia knew better than to argue with her now. She and Daisy would have to flee on their own, she resolved as she left the room.

MT followed her but thought better of it halfway down the hall and when she returned, a kitchen maid was sitting on the stool next to Jacob's bed. MT could smell that the girl had washed herself and crushed lavender into her hair. She had pulled off the scarf she wore tucked into her bodice, exposing her young, white cleavage. Though he was asleep, she leaned over him to kiss him, her lips inches from his face.

MT slammed her hands on the doorframe.

"Girl!" she barked, though she never called the maids that. "Get away from him!"

The young woman started, jumped to her feet, curtsied and fumbled to get her scarf tucked in again. She was tall and thin, with milky skin. The kind of woman MT had always wanted to be. The kind who sniggered behind her hand when she passed MT in the market.

"I'll not have…behavior of that sort going on in my house," MT said sharply.

The girl curtsied again and scurried out of the room without meeting MT's blazing eyes.

Jacob had not awakened from either the maid's advances nor the rap on the doorframe, so MT closed his door and stomped into the library. She leaned on the door, immobilized by the anger coursing through her. Not just anger, she realized, but panic as well. A completely foreign feeling. Fear mixed with an unreasonable rage that was bitter and sharp. She wanted to slap the woman or banish her. Not because she was the ideal shape and size, or that standing next to her, MT seemed even more distorted. What was this viciousness she was feeling? She had seen it in the markets, two women pulling at each other's hair. Kicking at each other. Was she jealous? Frightened that this lithesome maid would take Jacob away from her? Not that she had him. No, it was that a woman like that would use him, hurt him, treat him like a toy and then disappear. MT was protective, not jealous. She pushed off the door and ran her hands along the wall before she climbed into her desk chair. No. Jealous, not protective, she knew. Not that he was fragile or incapable. It's that he was different the way that she was different. Underappreciated. Denigrated. Underestimated. She wasn't his protector, she was his...what, she wondered. Friend? Companion?

In a way she envied the little world he had made of dancing rabbits and their little dresses, she thought, as she smoothed her hands over the flawless wooden desktop. His pillow mounds as cities. He had made his own joy, while she had lived stewing in the darkness of barren abbeys. He had used his imagination to build his own beautiful world while she had spent all her energy focused on how others denied her the world she wanted. Focused on what she didn't have, rather than building what she could. To her, he was glorious. Others might call him crazy or simple and infantilize him, but to her, he was inspiring. His whole life had been lived in childhood, while she had had none at all. She wanted to climb the hill and spend days sewing trim on the little dresses, making a special necklace for Julia the Flop-Eared. One thing was certain, she would protect him at all costs. From beautiful women who would use him, from marauders, and from the snickering of the cruel.

But the prospect frightened her, and she dug in the closet for the jug of wine and climbed into her bed, swigging from it until she slept.

~*~*~*~

In the morning, Percy came to the manor house to check on Jacob, but he sought out Claudia.

"How is he recovering?" Percy asked.

"We've stitched it and stopped the bleeding. Pray there's no fever," she said. "I wonder, could your big dogs guard the warren tonight?"

"Certainly. And I'll bring you some of the quail I bagged yesterday with the hunting dogs."

"A welcome rest from all the rabbit," she said.

Claudia was lightened, relieved. The discovery of Daisy's father removed any threat from Percy, and she regarded him with heightened interest. He was capable. Considerate. "Then I'll send you off with stew." She stepped closer and put her hand on his forearm. "To keep you warm."

Percy watched her walk down the hall to supervise the household. He had been talking to her all day in his mind, thinking of what she would advise about the sheep and chickens, seeing little Daisy running in the garden, Claudia's beautiful girth bending over the hearth, and imagining his child at her breasts.

Earlier in the day when he was returning from a hunt, he had found a sow and four piglets in a clearing in the woods and using a switch he cut and the dogs, coaxed them into a corral in the barn. He was pleased with himself when the sow laid down and the piglets latched on to nurse. Sheep, chickens, a cow, calf and now pigs, he recited to himself. A proper burgage, a proper farm. He wanted to describe it all to Claudia and hoped she would be impressed.

But when he went into the barn to hang up his tools in the late afternoon, he found one of the ratters dead just outside the pig's corral and found one of the piglets dead inside. He slammed the shovel against the wall and sat on a box. The sheep had been killed by the big dogs; piglets killed by the little dog who had been killed by the sow. He shook his head at his continuing misfortune. Or his continued ineptitude. And now he only had one ratter who would be less effective in chasing out the rabbits for slaughter. If this beautiful woman only knew what a failure he was.

Claudia, however, was relishing the kindness of Percy as she walked into the nursery, stepped around the maids' children and scooped up Daisy. The baby was not hungry, though, and fought against Claudia's insistent nipple so Claudia put her breasts away coarsely, glancing at the nursery girl to see if she had been a witness, then balanced the baby on her hip and left the nursery. The baby started to cry, having been awakened in the warm nursery but Claudia headed toward the kitchens where she was being summoned. The cook and kitchen maid both stood with their arms crossed over their chests, scowling.

"The upstart here thinks we've not enough food for all," Gertrude said disdainfully.

"All of us of the house, the baroness, the seamstresses, the old man and the young boy on the roof: she's miscounted by half," the teenage kitchen maid insisted as she ticked them off on her fingers.

"Besides," Gertrude continued, "we've nothing but rabbits. Rabbit stew, rabbits in gravy. Everything fried in coney fat."

Claudia sighed and bent over the stove. She lifted the lid of the pot, and a cloud of steam billowed across the baby's face.

The child screamed in pain and Claudia stepped back, the lid clattering on the floor.

"You'll kill that baby with all your fussing," Gertrude said, "and now look what you've done!"

Claudia grabbed a cloth from a drying rack as the baby screamed. She ran outside to the rain barrel and bathed the baby's face in the cool clean water, rocking her and weeping.

Claudia swaddled the girl tightly to keep her from pulling at the red-raw skin, crying as hard as her child.

Gertrude came up behind her and gave her a cloth.

"Use this," she said. "Vinegar will stop the burning."

Claudia quickly laid it on Daisy's skin, then tipped her up to prevent the vinegar from rolling into her eyes.

"I'm sorry for what I said," Gertrude said softly. She ran her sleeve over her forehead. "I had no right. It was…an accident. I just feel responsible…in my kitchen."

Claudia shook as she answered. "I've lost so many…" She looked at Gertrude, then looked away. "Four of my precious ones. Bad enough when they die inside you and you pray to expel them. The worst is when they are born but live just a few days. Just long enough to love them. Long enough to watch them suffer. I can't bear to…"

Gertrude put a hand on her shoulder. "We found some brandy. I'll bring a little for her, just to soothe her. And some for you."

Maybe she didn't deserve to be a mother, Claudia thought. All others dead and this one injured. What was she playing at? Maybe she *was* just her breasts.

CHAPTER TEN

Days later when the news of the prisoners' escape reached the earl, he woke with a raging hangover and bellowed about the treachery of the baroness.

"Those were *my* serfs, my workers! The first batch she kept for herself and now she's lost the second lot?" He paced the floor.

"There was an attack on the warren, your grace, and the robbers freed the prison…the serfs," his captain reported.

The marchioness sat forward. She had sent the thieves in; her manservant was selling the pelts in a town to the south and would return the money to her, not the earl, but her men would never have released prisoners. She pulled an old shawl tighter around her shoulders. To mention the marauders would expose her plan.

The earl bellowed at his captain. "We had an agreement! Head of a gorgon, that woman!"

"No longer, milord," his captain said. "I'm told that the sight of death all around her has softened her heart."

The earl scoffed. "Since we were children at court she's been a spiteful shrew. Well, I shall discover for myself. She and I need to… discuss our arrangement."

"Shall I prepare the carriage or your horse?"

"Neither," he said shortly, reconsidering his plan. He didn't relish the prospect of arguing with her. "I shall…consider the most appropriate time and…alert you." He resumed his pacing. His rank meant nothing when he stared into the mirrors on that damnable cap. It showed him cut into pieces by the swords of his enemies.

At dinner, the marchioness picked at an apple with a knife and considered her situation: the marauders had captured a scant half dozen pelts. If she couldn't have a large batch stolen, perhaps what she needed was a steady supply. Take the warrener himself. The warren on her brother's estate which was miles from the manor had fallen into disuse while her brother struggled with gout. Perhaps she could surreptitiously install the baron's warrener on her family's land. She could say that the simpleton had just wandered away. Tell him that he has been traded by the baroness and has an opportunity to develop a new coneygarth. She sipped her wine and wondered where her footman was.

~ * ~ * ~ * ~

On his third venture into town, Simon sat in the tavern growling into a black cloud of his own making. The nightmare of the boy, the arrow and the star-shaped wound had awakened him more times than usual. Upon falling asleep, the wound grew until Simon fell into it and woke up. When he slept again he saw an arc of arrows raining down ahead of him until gore swallowed him like quicksand. The ghost of the boy rose and pointed at the maw of the star-shaped wound, then to Simon's heart. No matter what carnage he had seen from this plague, no matter what cruelty he witnessed, it was the dream of the star-scarred boy that woke him in the night. He would give a kingdom for sleep, he thought each morning, for a witch to banish the ghost with elixir or poultice, a monk who could mumble absolution.

In the tavern, he grumbled and thumped his tankard on the table. The ale was too salty, the innkeeper had purposely brought him the worst piece of fish pie, and most of all, as he ground his back molars, the damnable sheriff had stolen his loot when he had been imprisoned. The sack of goods had bulged as he carried it, and he was nearly into town to cash in when he was surrounded by the sheriff and his rattling cage of emaciated men. He had been thrown in with the flea bitten and toothless while his sack was confiscated and hung on the sheriff's saddle. It had taken months for him to gather it and though the countryside was not as horrific as it had been when the sickness had first plowed through, it was a chore to find anything of value in this picked over, barren land.

On the other hand, his liberation at the hands of Empty the None had been proof of his own shrewdness. The months of watching her descend from pious nun to a numb and wordless grave digger had been worth the effort. She now promised him a reward for another load of stuff to outfit a manor house that was not hers and he would collect his earnings. Oh, he would certainly collect, though he was unsure of where her money had come from and how long it would last. But now the most important thing was to recapture the loot he had gathered and do whatever he could to insult the sheriff as he had been insulted. Building a jail to house men who demanded higher wages as was their God-given right in this depopulated land? He would see about that.

It took him almost until sundown to follow the innkeeper's rambling directions and arrive at the outskirts of the sheriff's encampment. Simon crouched in the weeds. This theft would require planning, and he didn't want to be out alone at night among the wolves. The horses were already becoming restless as they detected him. The jail was just a perimeter, with stones only as high as his calf, the mortar between them not set. Simon assumed that the prisoners were chained in a large tent and that the smaller tent, closer to the fire, housed the sheriff.

He hurried back to the inn and, in the morning, drove the load of MT's goods to the manor house but refused to unload it. He unhooked the wagon from the horse, ordered the boy to give it water and saddle it while Simon gathered provisions for his return to the sheriff's encampment. A crowbar to break the lock if there was a strongbox, a large sack or sheet to fill with booty if there was more to take, a long strip of something he could wrap around his head and face as a disguise. He needed to hit them after the noon meal when they were slower-witted and tired.

At noon, Simon tethered his horse in the forest and crept toward the encampment where the sheriff was shouting orders to the prisoners, his back to his tent. Simon, with his face fully wrapped so only his eyes were visible, crept to the edge of the tent listening for occupants, then he expertly slipped through the unsecured flap between the tent walls. Such easy pickings, he thought as he saw his sack of loot beside another, both stashed at the head of the sheriff's bed. Simon thought it was witless to leave the bags there, and picked up one in each hand, moving slowly so the contents did not jingle. He did not leave a fern bear. Not for this man. He backed out of the tent flap, smiling with satisfaction, but before he pivoted to run back to his horse, the sheriff stepped into Simon's view though without seeing Simon, and he stripped off his sweat-soaked shirt.

Simon froze in fear. A star-shaped scar on Baudwin's shoulder was gnarled and deep. There was no mistaking the shape and placement: it was the wound Simon fell into in his dreams, the scar that had devoured his nights. Here was the boy of his nightmares. Not dead. Alive. Simon dropped the bags, and they spilled their contents onto the grass as he backed away, more frightened of the ghostly boy than the sheriff's power. He ran to his horse, listening as the sheriff called for his deputies. Simon threw his scarf in the weeds and whipped the horse into a run.

~ * ~ * ~ * ~

MT was studying a map of the manor's crop rotation when Simon rushed into the library.

"You have to hide me," he said with a terror in his eyes that MT had never seen. "Where can you hide me?"

After all he had done, she was in no mood to grant him any favors. "Hide you? Not here. I won't have it."

"You owe me," he growled bending close to her ear. "Hide me!"

"Owe you?" she grumbled. "I owe you a skinning like the bear!" Before she could unleash her rage, though, she stopped and sighed with exasperation. If her heartless companion was this frightened, she reasoned, he was in serious trouble and MT wanted him as far away from the women of the manor as possible. Besides, he knew her secret. "Alright…the chapel. By the roadside. As a priest."

"Do I look like a priest?" Simon said looking down at his muddy boots and pants.

"Take all that off," she said as a plan formulated in her mind. She handed him the nightshirt. "You have taken a vow of poverty. The boots too."

"Barefoot?" Simon was flummoxed. "What do I do?"

"If anyone arrives lie down on your belly on the floor, arms out like the crucifix. You have a right to continue your prostration no matter what anyone does."

"What do I say?"

"The rosary!" She was met with a withering look. "Just repeat 'Hail Mary, full of grace' over and over. How dissolute are you?"

"Hail Mary, full of grace," he chanted tentatively.

"And put your hands together in prayer, any time you're standing. Don't let anyone see you on your way to the chapel."

Simon paced the chapel floor, kicking at the rubble of the broken and half-freed millstones with his bare feet. He was not a murderer. The relief tried to relax the muscles in his chest, but he pushed it aside. So what? He wasn't going to ride up and down on the terrain of enthusiasm. "Oh, look at the peak," the fools said, as if the valley wasn't below.

He laid down on his belly with his arms outstretched and wasn't sure if he was trembling because he was about to be punished as a thief, because he had actually seen the boy with the star-shaped scar or that he was nearly naked under a thin nightshirt with his chapped ass pointing at the door. Time stopped. He was unaccustomed to the quiet, the peace of the chapel and he felt he was in a trance-like state.

He didn't know how long he had been there when he was startled by the arrival of a young girl with a tray. She offered it with an awkward ceremony. He leapt up from the floor and wondered if he had actually been sleeping.

"Welcome to our manor, Father. Our lady hoped you would eat," the girl said, then looked around the chapel to see where the tray could be set down other than the altar. He gestured to the seat in the first row and the girl complied, trying not to look at his bare legs and knobby toes. He stepped away from her, embarrassed and uncertain of himself.

"Will you..." she said as she backed away, "...lead our prayers tonight? We have gone through so much, Father."

He waved her away, scowling. Pretending to be a priest was clearly not going to work, as he hadn't prayed in decades, and could no more lead Mass than turn himself into a laying hen, though he realized with a start that his life could depend on his charade. On the other hand, the girl seemed so frail. And the quiet in the chapel was having an inexplicable effect.

She backed away toward the door.

"Girl!"

She pivoted in fear.

"Tell your lady that… Father Benedict is cold. Bring me your best blankets."

"Yes, Father. Shall I clean the chapel for you?"

"No," he said sharply. He didn't want little girls flitting around. Especially if they were expecting prayers, from him of all people. "Bring me a broom and I shall… use it for my… meditation."

She left quickly, chastened. Simon walked the perimeter of the chapel digging leaves out of the nooks and scraping the mold off the statues, peering out the window for the sheriff. Simon had hidden before. He knew about the temporary disguise needed for an ambush or a sleight of hand; he knew all about the trickery of theft and the con. Somehow this was different. He tried again to convince himself that he was trembling because he was cold, but the reassurance was hollow. And he realized that he was frightened. More frightened than since the first time he ran onto the battlefield. If he was found he would be put to work or put in jail, at best, or mutilated and hung as a thief. But worst of all, the sheriff might exact the revenge of the wounded boy.

He gobbled down the soup and sat down, cross legged, behind the altar to shield himself from the draft from the door, or was it to hide the stripped-down man?

He ran his hands along the side of the altar in front of him, but suddenly realized that it was not a solid piece, it was a cupboard painted to look like stone with a knotted leather thong through a dozen peg holes. He fiddled with the knot, forced it open with his fingernails, and stripped the leather out, flinging it behind him. He opened the doors: orderly, clean, a priest's habit pressed, folded just so, a crude pewter goblet, an embroidered cloth for the altar and a well-worn Bible. He picked up the priest's habit, told himself that he would wear it against the cold, but as he put it on he was encircled by the surety of it, black, flawless, unadorned. Underneath the clothing in the cupboard was a knife. He paced outside and dragged the knife across his scalp, his thin black hair falling into the weeds beside the chapel. When he was completely bald, he put on the sash and stowed the knife in it.

As the hilt of the knife disappeared inside the sash, Simon saw MT charging toward him with a massive bundle of fur and a broom in her arms.

"Our best blankets?" she was furious. He hadn't seen her so overcome with rage since the bear's death. "Demand our best blankets? You want something warm? Wrap yourself in this!" She pressed the bearskin pelt into his arms and threw the broom to the ground. "Wrap yourself in your own cruelty."

"Is this from the...?" He ran his hands over the bearskin. The image from her cap was of arrowheads shooting back at him.

"You broke his heart. In all our wanderings, I never saw anyone weep like that, so you wear it like penance!" MT thought that with his head shaven, he looked like a wild animal. Amazing that the little girl who brought his tray didn't recognize him as the supply man. No one would recognize him now. It was one thing to gather supplies for them (no doubt taking a large cut for himself) but to make demands!

He slowly wrapped himself in the pelt, bowed his head, and pressed his palms together. "Mary, Mother of God," he pronounced and then mumbled it in repetition.

She was disgusted and gestured to his priest's garb. "Anything, even blasphemy, to save your own skin. Lucky for you the maids are begging me to invite you to supper. I told them of a priest's 'arrival.' See that you are not late." She sighed. "Any sign of the sheriff or whoever it is who is chasing you?

Simon shook his head. "I ran in the opposite direction of the manor and then doubled back," he said quietly.

MT turned on her heel and returned to the Manor. *Just what we need*, she thought as she stormed back up the hill. *More danger*.

That evening, the maids set Father Benedict a place at the head of the table which MT quickly occupied, resenting him before he had arrived. He imperiously entered in his black and white garb, using the bear pelt as a cape.

"Father." She gestured to the foot of the table and then sat down quickly in case he sat first.

The maids attempted to serve him before her. As MT guessed, his lack of hair and priestly garb was enough to fool the maids that he was not the sullen man they avoided when he brought supplies.

"We begin here," MT said sharply, pointing at her own

plate, then glaring at him. The baroness's reputation for rage was suiting her well now. The maids complied sheepishly, then scurried to stand against the wall. Even Gertrude the cook, who had protested over the staff eating in the dining hall, was wearing a clean apron and waiting for Simon to say grace.

"Perhaps…Father Benedict…would lead us in prayer," MT said acidly, even though she knew that unmasking him would unmask her. "On the topic of gratitude and kindness."

Simon could not meet her gaze even after their year of grizzly and immoral activities. He bowed his head. "Let us silently pray," he said, and all followed his lead. Despite his fear of capture, perhaps it was the end of the nightmare. The silence in his head unnerved him.

After dinner, MT insisted that he exchange the pelt for a blanket, and he returned to the chapel, bolted the door and spent hours chipping at the millstones embedded in the floor. Where are the answers? Where is forgiveness? What is justice, he wondered.

In the morning, a maid tapped lightly on the door and Simon stiffly rose from the pew where he had been sleeping. She handed him a mug of broth, then dropped to her knees.

"Forgive me, Father," she said softly.

He held himself rigid with surprise, then put the mug on the windowsill and led her to the front pew. They bowed their heads. "Hail Mary," he said, and she finished the rosary.

She was followed by another maid who slipped in as the other woman left. "Forgive me, Father."

The old man, the orphan boy, Gertrude the cook. All

morning, they trooped in to ask for the thing that he had rarely seen, was not empowered to give, and could not bring himself to request. After his charade, they rose and walked out of the chapel lightened and relieved, seemingly at peace, a condition that seemed odd to him. Two words was all it took? Forgive me. It was a demand, really. Would it work on his star-scarred ghost? The thought of asking the sheriff's forgiveness made him shudder.

Just before noon, MT burst into the chapel and glared at Simon with her hands on her hips.

Simon protested. "I can't do this."

"No, you can't. They will demand Mass from you on Sunday. I will announce that you are in silent reflection, not to be disturbed. I'll send the boy down with a small fire box, but you are not to speak to anyone, do you hear?"

"Gladly."

"Meals will be delivered. How long must we...endure this?"

"The sheriff must have ridden in the other direction."

At dusk, the marauders hired by the marchioness crept toward the warren through the back fields off a road that couldn't be seen from the manor house. They carried rope to tie up the warrener, stationed an extra horse to drape him across and because they were large men and they knew that Jacob was alone, they were surprised when they encountered the muscular fighting dogs that had been tied to the front door by Percy. The dogs snapped at the men and strained against their ties. No one could have entered, as this was the only door, and the windows were mere slits in the rock through which to shoot arrows. The bolt had been damaged during the last raid, however, and Jacob was so skittish since being injured and his very recent return to the lodge that he panicked and slid a long ladder from the second-story window to the ground, noisily clambered down and started running across the coneygarth. The marauders ran after him, closing the space between them while Jacob whimpered, and they tackled him just before a long expanse of raspberry bushes. Jacob wiggled free and ducked into the thorny patch, as he knew the thin trail that he and the rabbits took. The bandits tried to enter but cursed the bushes as they were cut. They hacked at the bushes with their swords until they saw Jacob sprinting toward a small grove of trees. Jacob tip-toed over the labyrinth of exposed and hardened roots under which the rabbits made their home. This was Matilda's queendom, and he knew it well but didn't stay. He ran on toward Eleanor's land. Following him into the grove, the marchioness's front-runner caught his foot on a tree root, and he fell, grabbing his ankle in pain.

MT later decided that it was because they were all in the chapel for evening prayers that they didn't hear the dogs and the kidnapping of Jacob. MT had flatly told the maids that there were no wine or wafers, that Father Benedict's preference for silent prayers were the best that could be done but they paced down to the roadside chapel anyway. MT was there to be sure that Simon, as Father Benedict, didn't attempt Latin, make outrageous promises or tithe these women who had nothing. Percy was there because Claudia was.

When they heard the dogs barking, though, MT ordered Claudia to protect the women and Percy ran up the hill. MT followed and when she got to the lodge, Percy had climbed the ladder in the back and shouted down that Jacob was gone. He quieted the dogs and opened the door for MT, who frantically checked for signs of a struggle or blood. In the distance, they saw one of the marauders helping his limping compatriot cross the field toward the road and thought they were seeing Jacob being dragged by his captor. Percy lit out after them, running diagonally toward the road and didn't hear MT suggesting that he should get the horse for the pursuit.

MT bent double and put her head in her hands. They had lived under near constant threat: having survived almost certain death from contagion, then freed from imprisonment and pending slavery, scraping a meal together in a ransacked house and abandoned garden, fighting off men intent on enslaving them again, only to face greed and theft, a full-on assault against the warren, and now a targeted campaign against a beloved man. All while they were engaged in deception if not kidnapping of their own, plus crimes against the king and blasphemy, she thought, turning toward the chapel.

She and Percy were going to split up to cover more ground in their search, but Percy insisted that she wasn't safe alone. Merek and the orphan boy arrived to make a second team, and since Jacob would not be hiding in the open fields, if he had escaped at all, they set out to investigate every stand of trees in the coneygarth. They called to him, the wind blowing their words back at them as they trudged the property. Merek returned to her, convinced that Jacob had been taken, and Percy reluctantly agreed. She scanned the fields, her eyes following the ribbons on their pegs, and had an idea.

"You go back and…check that all are safe. I have an idea. If I'm wrong, Percy, you can take the horse and ride to the village to ask after him."

When she was certain that she couldn't be seen, MT ducked into the thicket and scurried to the cottage. She called softly to him as she opened the door and found Jacob wrapped in the rabbit fur blanket, hiding under the bed. When he tentatively emerged on his knees, she grasped his cheeks, kissed his forehead and he encircled her in the fur blanket. She threw her arms around him, and they clung to each other in relief.

CHAPTER ELEVEN

In the morning, Percy struggled, again, to milk the cow while the calf who was penned in the corner lowed in protest. This plan to better himself was a fool's errand. *What does a dog boy know about farming?* he lamented again, in an almost daily diatribe. Apparently watching from afar hadn't taught him enough to actually succeed. He managed to get sheep here because they were docile and too afraid of the dogs to venture outside the herd, but he had only watched them being shorn and certainly could not butcher them. Between feeding the horse, the dogs and him, there were now hardly any vegetables to transplant. Yesterday he had planted the saplings but was convinced that he had let the root balls dry out and that they were sure to die or, at the very least, struggle to produce fruit for several years. He had been sent to the baron's household so young that he had never had so much as a kitchen garden let alone grown a crop so what would the horse and the cows eat if the next winter was harsh? He knew he was very good with dogs but apparently not with any animal that could not be trained, could not be told what to do and expected to do it. Now that Claudia knew of their return, he would have to turn over the dogs to the baroness, though with a manor house as barren as it seemed, she probably had no need for the fighting dogs. The hunting dog who had dropped rabbits and quail at his feet during their journey could certainly be of use. So here he was, dependent on his care of dogs again.

Claudia had been watching him from a corner of the barn with a bowl of soup covered with a cloth. With irritation, she shoved the bowl into his hands. "What did you think? That all you had to do was possess the animals? Farming is hard work! Now eat that before it gets cold. I'll show you." She hiked her skirts up and squatted on the stool, the milk zinging into the pail.

The land was not as generous as Percy assumed, she thought. The cow stamped her hoof as Claudia pulled too hard on her teat. After the Great Mortality everyone knew to their marrow that life could strike you down regardless of whether you were capable or wealthy or your animals were the finest in the county. Was this man strong enough to admit his shortcomings and not slink away from them? Or was he wrestling with the angel, too frightened to acknowledge his success? Regardless, she wasn't going to confide in him. If she told Percy her story, revealing the babies who had perished, she would weep. Describing the failed farm, the fleeing husband and her move to the baroness's house would reveal her as the wet nurse, alert him to Daisy's origin, and unravel the whole deception. She turned back to the bucket silently and dampened her irritation.

"Are the hens laying yet?" she asked him quietly.

"No," he said with a sigh. "Not yet. I'm very sorry to hear about Daisy's injury."

Claudia stopped milking.

"The baron would not tolerate a dog with scars," he said, seeing her shoulders slump, "so I kept lavender oil on hand. First stop the burning with an acid like verjuice or green grapes, crab apples, sorrel."

"I've done that."

"Then lavender oil right on the skin," he said. "I'll look for some growing when we finish here."

She hung her head and wept, leaning her forehead on the flanks of the cow. He crouched beside her and put his arm around her shoulders.

"I've never had a child, but…" he said quietly, thinking of the horror when his first dog had been kicked, the pain when a member of the pack broke its leg or the look in their eyes as they lay confused over a fever, and all the while looking to him for solutions and strength. Offering their devotion and loyalty until the very moment they passed. "But pain. Fear. Guilt. Seems to me it's all part of love."

Merek avoided the bakery in the manor house and spent his time in the kitchen, tending the fire as if courting Gertrude. She was not easily won over, however.

"You can't trust skinny bakers," she said, looking him over. "Means they put sawdust in the flour."

He nodded knowingly, kept his secret to himself but was impressed that she could tell he was no baker. The knot of resentment toward his mother tightened further in his chest.

"Did you know that on the continent they have forks at each place setting?"

Gertrude scoffed. "An unmanly affectation. The bishop says that God in his wisdom has provided us with natural forks – our fingers – and it would be an insult to Him to substitute them with these metallic devices."

Merek smiled at her and changed the subject to the heat and length of burn from different woods, of fires he had seen going for months; fires that shed no light; fires that made the ground steam; entire villages going up in flame and bogs that spontaneously ignited on the Solstice. He wanted to tell her about all the fires that had the same color as her hair but kept his appreciation to himself.

While she cooked and barked orders, Merek described the entourage of the king, the wild times at the world's largest market, fairies in the forest who blessed the dead.

"You work for Baroness Liberty," he said absently, and she cocked her head, surprised.

He put another log on the fire and asked her if it was burning too hot. Had she seen that new invention, the sawmill? Amazingly fast. Does in a day what would have taken weeks. He restacked kindling. A rich man in Oxford was the first to use science to forecast weather. There was a motherless child who sewed little bags to float above a fire at festivals. Did she know anyone who wore spectacles right on their face and not as hand-held glass?

Gertrude generally didn't like people in her kitchen, but his stories were intriguing, so she welcomed him, gave him bits of roasted rabbit and saved him crackling fish skins. The kitchen maids grinned behind their hands, relieved that Gertrude was less surly when Merek was around. Gertrude looked into his blue eyes longer every day and asked him to describe his best recipes for pies and crusty bread. Merek waved her question away: without flour there was no point in discussing it, he said. Besides, he didn't like to talk about himself. Pride cometh before a fall, it's said, and he steered the conversation in a different direction. Lute playing was certainly popular now. Had she heard one? Had she ever cooked for a house that had one? She gave him a big mug of steaming rosemary tea as she sat on a stool and rubbed her hands, ready for his next story.

Merek knew he was being disingenuous. He told of other people's accomplishments, travels and conquests, while he had none of his own. A magician's trick, sleight of hand, diverting attention from his own uselessness.

With a long pause, he asked her. "Have you ever heard of Prester John?" A Nestorian king, he intoned with a flourish, who ruled over a Christian nation lost amid the pagans and Muslims of the Orient. Gertrude stirred the pot with a small smile. No one could find it, Merek said, though vast fleets of ships had been sunk trying to find him, which was a fact, undeniable. The kitchen maids gathered behind Gertrude to hear as he spun his story out in great detail, though it now sported his own embellishment. He described the riches that spilled from the windows of the palace into a heap of jewels below, waterfalls that descended from the clouds amid trees that floated without roots. Horses had two heads that could never be pointed in the same direction and so were useless for transport, but dogs were so smart that they taught children to read. There were birds of nine colors and in Prester John's land dragons had just recently been conquered, a tale of heroism for another day, he said. As Prester John was a descendant of the Three Magi, he would be discovered and honored one day, Merek was sure of it.

Gertrude waved the maids back to work and tucked her hair deeper into her kerchief. She asked him again about his baking. He described the new college at Cambridge founded three years ago; predicted great success for the first commercial weaving – not just women for their family, this was a big operation, a business that had just begun in York.

Merek took delight in Gertrude's interest, but also in the fond memory of the people who had given him the story. He had learned about the fork from a ladies' maid who had returned from France and longed for an English bap. Scientific advances were described by a monk with no front teeth while he drank in a tavern and the ale dribbled from the corners of his mouth. Old men spotting a place where their memories might be honored sat on benches near the warm oven and picked their teeth as they narrated. Scholars debated at the side of his oven; tradesmen recounted frightening turns of fortune; housemaids who balanced a day's worth of dough balls on a tray on their head passed along news of the wars that used their brothers as cannon fodder. On his route he stopped at the same monastery and tavern to gather updates before he stopped at markets where his oven was in demand.

Gertrude sent the remaining kitchen maids to prepare the head table and when they were gone, she stepped to Merek, who stood.

"I hope they never find flour," said Gertrude quietly, "so your stories never end."

MT came into the kitchen and Merek took a small step away from Gertrude and couldn't hear what MT was saying to the cook. Merek towered over MT, and in her cap he saw a mixed-up world outside the world, and it beckoned to him. Like Gertrude, he hoped it was a world without flour.

The next morning the kitchen maids pressed him for another story. "Well," he said, giving the coals a last rake and, remembering the look of MT's black cap near his fire the night before, he began. "There was a woman named Baroness Hearth Fire who was warm and loving unless poked and then she would flare up and consume whole villages. One day…"

At the end of the day, Gertrude dismissed the kitchen maids while Merek lingered near the hearth, and she sat down in front of him. "I've always wanted," she started, then hung her head and glanced over her shoulder. "To cook for people who mattered. Not just simple fare for us working folk." She gestured behind her to the house. "A great, stuffed pig on a platter. A swan, peacocks. A boar's head in pepper sauce. Can you imagine?" She leaned toward him, then ran a towel through her fingers. "To have so much pepper that you can put gobs of it in a sauce! To have dates and oranges, quinces and cranes. I hear in the palace there are sometimes twenty dishes served at a meal. Twenty! They make sausages with spices from the Far East. What I wouldn't give for the queen to hold a bowl of my soup to her lips and savor it. That would be a triumph. My food among the fine brocades. Soup from my kitchen served in a gold tureen with bejeweled spoons."

Merek smiled as he had while listening to the secrets of the village women. Her face had lost its surly disappointment: it was lit up. He gently took her hand in his, a bold move that he hoped wasn't too forward. He took stock of the cook's burns on her arms: some long and thin from the edge of a pan, some round and deep from a flying coal, a few amorphous and shallow from a sauce that had gotten away from her. She looked at their hands, raised her face to his eyes, and took the stub of his shortened arm in her other hand. He looked down, then back at her with surprise.

"You must long to bake with cinnamon and nutmeg," she said softly to change the subject.

"And sugar," he said, recovering himself but not moving his arm. "It has sweetness with no color or flavor, unlike honey."

"No flavor?"

"None. Brought from Italy or Al-Andalus. I hear it crunches between your teeth like salt."

~ * ~ * ~ * ~

That afternoon, Claudia entered the library just moments before the sheriff.

"They've hung the maid who had some of the pelts," Claudia said and choked back tears as she turned on her heel and left.

The sheriff strode into the library with several rabbit pelts over his arm.

After a brief bow of his head, he held out the pelts to MT. "Returning your goods, milady. Assuming they're yours, as you have the only warren around. The thief has been…dealt with."

MT said nothing but grimly climbed the stairs to her desk chair. She motioned for the sheriff to lay the pelts in a chair. The woman's death was her fault, tempting a woman who had nothing. And if MT screamed in his face like she wanted, her own death would follow. She waved the sheriff away and he bowed out of the room.

Two hours later, Claudia came into the library and found MT on her knees polishing the wainscoting in symmetrical white circles using a bees wax treatment they had found yesterday. Claudia whispered urgently to her, but she didn't respond, and Claudia quickly closed the door behind them. MT didn't turn, just moved her rags and the crock of polish down a few inches, moved herself on her knees, began more polish circles.

Claudia sighed and hung her head, then backed out of the room without a word. They had been in the manor house two weeks, but the sheriff still hovered nearby. When were they going to be safe enough to flee?

Unfortunately, a maid got a glimpse of MT on her knees before Claudia entered the library, which drew a whole clutch of maids to the door when Claudia left the room. She barked at them to return to work, but the damage had been done: either the baroness had gone mad, or this was no baroness, they whispered among themselves. Don't forget her attendance to the handsome, childish warrener. MT now seemed dangerous. Royals are treacherous but people with very little other than their ambitions and pretensions of royalty are the most dangerous of all. A woman who would lie about herself (even though she had rescued them from degradation), was a woman who could be expected to lie again. The staff inspected the flatware before dinner and determined it to be worthless. They reminded themselves of the lack of fine candlesticks or tapestries that could be sold in the market. MT shifted in their minds from their savior to a suspect.

Three days after Simon's visit to the encampment, the sheriff's posse rode down the hill and stopped at the chapel. The pounding horse hooves could be felt through the floor and the closed door. Despite the punishment to come, Simon had lost the will to run into the woods or dodge danger as he always had. There was no point in trusting his priestly disguise: he was sure his guilt would unmask him.

Baudwin walked without the authority or aggression that Simon expected.

"Forgive me, Father," the sheriff said with a catch in his throat as he dropped to one knee. He clutched his hands together tightly. "Forgive me, please."

Simon was shocked. The women had assumed forgiveness was something he could dispense, but he had no idea what it even was. He had seen it from a mother and an errant child, her hands on hips then flooded with…what was it, tenderness? There was no forgiveness in his world: a war is fought to the last man. Nobles might be captured and spared but there was no fate but death for the likes of his kind. Watching the blacksmith, he could see that even fathers kept tally before forgiving. They might feed you and make room under the blanket at night but there was a list, and it never got shorter.

"I hung her," Baudwin said. "By the road, I hung her for having a pelt. Clearly a thief. I was chasing down someone else, a man who tried to steal from my tent but there she was. A thief. The law is on my side, Father. But her eyes!" The sheriff hung his head. "Without a second thought, I had her hung."

Listening to the sheriff, Simon didn't think of the temporary reprieve his disguise was giving him. It deepened his guilt, added insult to injury to pretend to give absolution. They hadn't seen each other eye to eye but Simon was still surprised that he hadn't been recognized as one of the captured men. More than that, he was struck dumb by the plea for forgiveness from the man whose forgiveness he craved.

"We shall pray together," Simon said, "silently…for forgiveness."

Baudwin gripped Simon's hands as they prayed. "The lass

is not here for me to beg forgiveness. She must have gone to her death hating me. How can I live with that, Father?"

It was a question that Simon had asked himself for years and it made Simon's own confession press against the inside of his teeth.

"Do you know...forgiveness?" Simon hoped it sounded rhetorical, not the question of someone who had no understanding of it.

"Once, on a battlefield when I was just 12 years old, I was injured but not severely and I lay there watching the clouds when a boy my age came up and stabbed me in the shoulder. I've been thankful to him every day since."

"Thankful?" Simon twisted sharply in his seat.

"He was an enemy, and his job was to kill me, but he didn't. He just stabbed me in the shoulder. I wouldn't be here today if it hadn't been for his kindness."

Simon crumpled over their clasped hands and closed his eyes. Here was his absolution. The stabbing had been his first act of barbarism, the first darkness that had clung to him thereafter. Now he was forgiven. The sheriff called it an act of kindness and had felt mercy long ago. How could that be? Of course, he hadn't actually confessed, he countered. The sheriff might not have...no, surely would not have forgiven him if he had known he had been face-to-face with his attacker. No one had that much generosity, though he reminded himself that it had just been extended to him.

Isn't that what he had always wanted, a reprieve from the star-shaped wound? Some way to wipe the gore from his dreams? Simon debated with himself. Who knew if this would stop the nightmares or banish the ghost of the boy? It was foolish drivel, all this priestly yack-yack. People are cows, mooing at carvings and pictures. His priestly disguise had to hold, though, because there were so many things to hide: his identity as a man in the jail; as a thief who had tried to recover his loot from the sheriff's tent; and worst, as the boy who had stabbed another without remorse. Not to mention the crime of impersonating a priest. And a nagging voice in the back of his head told him that exposing his identity would ruin a lifetime of gratitude that had powered Baudwin: the sheriff believed that his impaling had been an act of kindness and that had probably made Baudwin a gentler man who believed there was goodness in people. Fool, he thought, but would it be unkind to strip him of that? *Who cares*, he thought. But Simon wanted forgiveness for himself, didn't he? *Yes*, he thought. *No*, he countered. What good would it do? Why join the herd of the happy?

He tightened his grip on the sheriff's hands and the two bowed their heads again. Simon muttered under his breath and the sheriff believed that what he couldn't hear was the incantation that he wanted to hear.

"Thank you, Father," Baudwin said plaintively, with a gratitude that set Simon's teeth on edge.

Simon spent half of the night chipping at the millstones in the floor. He hammered viciously at the surrounding cement, then stopped as if frozen. He curled onto a pew to sleep then threw off the thin blanket and went back to the millstones. Exhausted, he fell into a dreamless sleep. No wound, no stabbing, no quicksand or ghost. Blackness. Blankness. Silence. He woke covered in sweat with scratches on his arms. No dreams of carnage or crows. A soundless night. A longed-for silence, wasn't it? No. A horrifying void. Was blissful sleep just the void of delusion? He tried to scoff at the idea, to think his way out of this but couldn't. Here was what he had always wanted: the end of the torment. How many times had he banged his head on the wall of the inn trying to stop the voices? And now the sheriff had rid him of...his only companion. Without the ghost boy he didn't even have the incessant voice of guilt.

He woke at daybreak after just an hour of sleep more frightened than he had ever been. More alone. The torment by the ghost boy had justified his worldview. Excused his loathing of others. What did he have now? Nothing. He wasn't a murderer, but he wasn't...anything.

And he certainly wasn't a priest. Couldn't even pretend to give absolution. The thought of another doe-eyed maiden coming to confess felt like an impending shower of nails.

Simon fled in the morning, and a young woman bringing his breakfast reported that the altar was dotted with two dozen little fern bears and the millstones half-freed from the floor.

CHAPTER TWELVE

Late that afternoon, huge storm clouds darkened the skies and made it seem much later than it was. When the rain started, the maids stood at the windows watching the puddles, pointing out the glistening leaves and sparkle on spider webs, the patter on the cobblestones, how all colors deepened, and the ground seemed thirsty. They accomplished little that day, and the household took to their beds early, considering it a justifiable holiday.

In the night when the rain pelted harder than they could remember, several women resolved to look for damage in the morning: for leakage in the storerooms, make sure that the chickens all had dry bedding out of the rain, check the herbs in the kitchen garden. The women turned over to sleep again. All slept late, as very little sunshine broke through the rain, and when guilt and habit finally drew them from their beds, they were drawn first to the windows to see that the downpour continued.

The kitchen maid poured mugs of broth for all as they stood silently at the windows.

Claudia sent a boy out to check the wood pile and ordered that fires should first be laid in the baroness's library, then the nursery, the central hearth in the Great Room where she moved the seamstresses, and the servants' quarters only at the very end of the day. The kitchen hummed regardless of the weather, as Gertrude was quick to point out, and the smell of a hearty rabbit stew lifted their spirits, though some grumbled that it was rabbit, again. It rained all day. MT was pleased that at least it meant that no prisoners would be delivered.

They went to bed remarking on the weather and slept well but in the morning when the deluge continued, they began to worry. Claudia, her size and softness comforting in itself, moved serenely through the staff, chiding them for their nervousness. "It's just a little rain," she said.

All the children were anxious and whining. Claudia checked that the nursery was warm enough and that Daisy's feet were covered, and she prayed that the burn across the child's cheek would continue to fade from red to pink. MT was outside in her oil cloth cape and boots, wading through the flooded courtyard and conferring with the old man on how to open the gate to drain the water without eroding the lane. The chickens were dry enough, though in their fear had not laid any eggs.

MT ordered that rain barrels be set out to capture the abundance – good for cooking, for water troughs, for the bath – but by mid-morning they were spilling over. Merek suggested firing up a smoker that sat idle under the eaves so they could preserve the remaining fish and rabbit.

"It's bound to end soon," MT told anyone who asked, but called the boy sentry and the old man from their post. No one would be arriving in this weather.

It rained a week without stopping and on the first morning of the second week, MT stood under the eaves with Gertrude and Claudia, watching the water pour over the edges of the raised beds and take the topsoil with it. The bean poles had toppled over. The roots of even the low-lying courgettes were exposed.

Merek joined them under the eaves. "Reminds me of the rain of 1314," he said solemnly. The three women turned to him. "Rained for five months. Without a break."

"Five!" Gertrude gripped Merek's arm in alarm and hurried back to the kitchen.

Claudia predicted that unless the rain stopped soon, all of the barley would be lost. If the rain battered down the alfalfa and it rotted in the mud, it would be lost as well. When would they be able to harvest?

They were all numb from the rain that trapped them indoors and washed away their work until MT came striding down the hall. "Bring in the root balls…Anything that hasn't been torn to shreds. Wrap them in…" She was at a loss for what to do.

"Yes," Claudia brightened. "We'll wrap them in damp fabric, and we'll replant when the rains stop." They were relieved to have a task, a way to fight the rain and the feeling of helplessness.

That evening, Merek sat in front of the fire in the Great Room and began a story of the rain and floods of 1314. Five months of rain, he told them, a year without a summer, without crops. But when he began to tell them of the famine that had descended on the countryside afterward, MT interrupted him.

"Baker," she said sternly.

Merek cleared his throat, shifted the logs and began again. "Who among you have seen the game of tennis? In 1308 the French king had a court – a tennis court – built indoors. And just this year, we English have moved it outdoors, though clearly no one played it today! It uses what's called a racket."

Later that evening, MT summoned Merek to the library. "Tell me about the rain of 1314." She paced the floor.

Merek bowed his head then straightened his shoulders. "People went mad from the sound of it. Sheep knocked off their feet and drowned in the torrent. It washed all the good soil into the rivers. Without a summer and without the soil, the famine was unlike anything anyone had seen."

"How long did you say it rained?"

"Five months."

"Five! That's impossible." She wished she had something to chew on. A bone, a turnip, anything.

"I have it on good authority. The scribes of York. I'm sorry but it is written."

"We are under siege!" MT shook her head. "Five months! What did the survivors do?"

"Milady?"

"The smart ones. The ones who made it through. What did they do?"

Lightening cracked in the sky and Merek saw it flash

across the mirrors in MT's cap like a sharp command. The rain of 1314 had always just been a story, popular with his customers because it involved people in unthinkable jeopardy. He hadn't thought about how to survive it.

"I am a simple...fire-tender," he said.

"There's nothing simple about you, Merek," she said sternly. "Based on your stories, you are one of the most intelligent people I've met. We must all... stretch ourselves to be our very best now."

Merek looked at the floor and considered. "I would start with the wood," he said.

They inspected the woodpile, and MT was glad that she had brought it inside the walls of the manor grounds. She had considered it protected beneath its makeshift roof, but when they inspected it the water and mud was now so deep that the bottom logs were soaked, and the rest of the pile was wet. No one could chop more wood in the rain but if they had no fire there would be no cooking, no warmth, no health.

"Where have we stockpiles?" she asked.

"The bakery, the brewery, the Great Room and the kitchen," Merek said. "Small ones in your room, the nursery, the servants' quarters."

"Let's get these inside, and consolidate the rest," she said. MT ordered that all the tables in the bakery be moved against the wall and that everyone, including the seamstresses, bring the wood inside to line the other wall, leaving a small walkway from the door to the large clay oven. With all the fires being laid in the house, the pile looked like enough for another month, a month and a half if the stockpile in the brewery was as large. But no woodpile would last forever.

MT summoned Claudia, Gertrude and Merek to the library.

"I fear we have a challenge ahead and while we pray it is not like the rain of 1314, we must bend our minds to survival. Consolidation. Using as little as possible to last the longest. Food made with small fires and all parts used," she said to Gertrude. "Candles treated as precious."

"And no fire in the servants' quarters," Claudia offered. MT looked nervous at the suggestion. "Send them to bed with hot rocks wrapped in cloth, milady."

"Yes, alright. I solicit any plans from you as to how to protect ourselves. If the rain stops soon we will be glad to be prepared for worse, and if the worst comes we will be glad to have started our preparations early."

The next morning MT found the maids at the upstairs windows, watching a rake and a hoe floating toward the wall of the house.

"The river's nearly breached the bank," a maid said breathlessly. "Bridge will be underwater soon."

Claudia thought of Percy: if the bridge was nearly underwater, the farm was sure to be flooded. Borrowing MT's cloak even though it was far too short, she gingerly made her way down the hill to his farm, and she found him in his barn with the water up to his ankles, checking the hooves of the bleating sheep. All his animals were out of the downpour but miserable and cold in standing water. The dogs sat shivering on top of wooden crates and the horse raised her legs one after another in agitation.

He brightened to see her, then turned back with chagrin to his farm. "The house is flooded as well," he said.

"Then you must come to the manor. You can't stay here." She waded across the barn to his side.

"I can't leave them," he said, gesturing to his herd.

She smiled to herself over his devotion. "The manor doesn't have a barn," she said. "Our stables are for horses, not wide enough for cows, I don't think."

He turned back to the sheep.

"Bring the horse," she said. "And the dogs. Let's see what the manor has. Milady is generous and would not want you to suffer."

He shook his head sadly as he surveyed the wreckage. "I should have known this wouldn't work."

She grabbed his arm. Her husband had surrendered to bad luck. Would this one buckle as well? "Did you make this rain? Cause the flood?"

He looked into her eyes, stunned. He picked up her hand and kissed her knuckles. They stood quietly with their hands entwined.

"I'll stay at the manor house just until the rains stop," he said quietly.

"I can carry the ratter under my cloak," she said and strode to the crates. The hunting dog bounded down and searched Percy's face for his orders. Percy put the cow and calf into a stall, backed the horse up and told the sheep of his return before closing them in.

"You talk to your sheep?" Claudia said with mirth. "They're much dumber than dogs, you know."

Percy smiled at her jibe and shrugged his shoulders.

It was slippery going. Claudia used the stairs cut into the hill and Percy nearly fell as the horse sensed her destination and trotted up the hill toward the gate. Once in the stall, the horse shook off the rain and Percy threw a blanket over her back, then turned to assess the other stalls. "Maybe not too narrow if we take down the middle slats. Would the baroness mind if…"

"Do it!" Claudia said and looked around for a hammer.

The cow and calf were more difficult to move, and Percy fell in the mud several times before he got them into the stables.

He turned to immediately to go to his sheep.

"Come in and get dry and warm first," Claudia said. "We can't have you falling ill." He looked down at his muddy, rain-soaked pants and agreed.

Claudia took him to the kitchen fire and ordered the staff to feed him. She strode into the library to confer with MT.

"Yes, very sensible," MT said when told of the horse and cow now in the stables.

"There's a flock of sheep, a sow and her piglets, though," Claudia said. "At the very least we need to get them up the hill and out of the water. They'll get sick and die if they stand there much longer. Let alone if the river floods and they are washed away."

Settling the sheep into the outbuildings, Percy was grateful. Sheep had saved him as a child. During a brutal winter, when Percy was trembling in his mother's arms despite being wrapped in her cape and every blanket they had, his mother stood with resolution and carried him, bent against the wind, toward the village sheep barn. Halfway there, they ran into a neighbor. Percy's mother shouted over the wind, gestured toward the sheep barn but the woman, with her baby swaddled in her arms, sneered at Percy's mother, too good to sleep among animals. In the barn, his mother quickly stacked the bales of hay against the walls to block the cold, packed the herd into a corner of the barn and bade them to lay down. Percy and his mother laid down in the middle and, surrounded by the thick wool and frosty breaths of the ewes, they were so warm that steam was rising from them and the animals when they woke in the morning. Elsewhere in the hamlet, an old man died after coughing for an afternoon; the next night several of the women slept together in a single house with the bed moved nearly into the fire but still trembled from the cold, and when Percy and his mother headed toward the sheep barn again, the neighbor ridiculed them for their smell, how they lived one step above the beasts, that she would rather die than fall that low. She got her wish: her baby died the following night and thereafter she turned away from Percy's mother whenever their paths crossed.

He had been saved by sheep, was devoted to dogs, now dedicated to saving sheep in return.

That afternoon MT was conferring with Merek and Percy when they heard a huge crash. They rushed to the back windows where they saw a wagon that had skidded downhill and crashed into the garden wall. They would need the wagon when they escaped, MT thought, for the first time planning their departure, and as part of a now nearly panicky hoarding of tools, livestock and food. Following them into the rain and across the garden to the wall, she ordered Merek and Percy to unseal the garden door and situate the wagon parallel to the wall.

"We must protect the back door," Percy shouted above the deluge, but mud gathered at the wall's edge threatened to seal it. The two men gestured to one another, then described their plan to her with hand motions and unheard words. She nodded more from trust than knowledge and they tipped the wagon over on its side so that the wheels were braced on either side of the garden door and the flatbed diverted the water and mud around it. They could open the back garden door but would have to climb over the wagon to leave the compound.

Merek and Percy steadied MT between them as they trudged through the garden, bent against the rain, the water up to their ankles and her knees. They strained to open the door to the manor house that swung outward but as soon as they crossed the threshold they saw that the water they were letting in was pouring into the kitchen, so MT ran over and slammed the door, cutting off the cook and maids who began shrieking inside. The water rose up the stairs until MT's dress floated and she scurried up the steps just enough to stay safe. While Merek strained to close the door, Percy opened the parallel door to the courtyard and the water poured in, which made the livestock protest.

MT descended the steps as the water drained into the courtyard. They would be vulnerable if she opened the main gate, though she doubted anyone was out in the deluge.

No one had ever seen rain like this. So relentless. So destructive and in keeping with their belief that it was the End of Days. First a plague. Then a deluge. Gertrude went to the window several times a day expecting to see a shower of frogs.

MT wouldn't allow anyone to go down the hill to the chapel and Simon the priest was gone, so they had no one to pray with them, no one to lead the plea for intersession. MT refused to do it though she knew how, telling herself it was to protect her identity, but it was really because she didn't believe in it anymore. Let them pray by themselves; MT was focused on finding a practical solution to their problem.

There were still no eggs, and Gertrude wouldn't jeopardize the health of her maids by sending them to the dovecote. The water stood inches deep around the base of the biggest tree on the hill that might shelter the sheep, but they would starve if kept dry in the corral. Percy and Claudia started rationing the feed for the sheep who bleated all day in their hunger.

The corral where the prisoners had been kept was flooded and useless, and the water continued to rise.

That afternoon a flock of white ducks descended on the courtyard as if it was a pond. MT, Merek and Percy – soaked, muddied and a little panicked – stood in the water in appreciation of the birds' flawless white feathers and serene movements.

"Do we have a net?" MT asked quietly.

Merek nodded. "Duck will give us a rest from all the rabbit."

Percy fetched the fishpond net that had floated to the back

door of the house and slowly waded into the courtyard. He bagged one of the birds and was surprised that the flock didn't take to the wing to escape.

"Weather too bad even for ducks," MT called brightly.

Percy smiled but reminded her. "We can't have the livestock in standing water."

MT heard banging on the kitchen door. "Nor the cook imprisoned at the hearth. Open the main gate. But try to bag another duck before they go."

Percy waded toward the gate while MT put her hands on her hips and turned to survey the new courtyard pond. A flock of Mallard ducks descended as well. Merek thought that they looked like emeralds among the pearls of the ducks and the diamond glint of MT's cap. For a small flock of passing swans, though, the glass on MT's cap looked like silvery fish and they descended, snapping at her head with their long beaks and nearly covering her under their wingspan. She shrieked and flung her arms up, so they redirected their ferocity toward the other birds and chased the ducks into a stall that held the chickens.

Aided by the pressure of the water, Percy opened the front gate and was nearly upended by its rush downhill. The livestock shook their manes and stomped their hoofs, but the ducks didn't leave. Claudia threw open an upstairs window.

"Put out more bedding for the ducks so they don't chase the chickens off their roost," she called to Percy. "And it's better to chase off the swans than let them bully the rest."

Percy beamed up at her despite the rain and hoped his future would include her.

With a wave of his arms, the swans lifted into the air despite the rain but were found later that day swimming on the fishpond in the flooded back garden.

In the kitchen, Gertrude leaned both hands on the table, crying quietly. A young maid stood at her elbow. "Rabbit. Again," Gertrude said, not with the indignation of the previous weeks but with sorrow and resignation. "Rabbit and eggs. Fish and eggs. Soon no eggs." *Not a cook to a royal. Just peasant food.*

MT startled them as she spoke from the entryway. "You understand how important you are here, Gertrude, do you not? We are spending a lot of time on conserving wood, but your work is even more important."

Gertrude whirled around, looked down and curtsied, fingering the edge of her apron. The young maid beside her kept her eyes downcast.

MT understood the feeling of settling for something beneath one's ability. "Our lives depend on your skill. Not in creating fancy dishes or beautiful things. It's even more crucial than that: making our meager food stores last as long as possible."

Gertrude straightened herself but kept her head bowed.

MT continued. "True, it's rabbit, again. Out of a stew pot. Not presented with the flourishes you no doubt could give it, but making our food outlast the rain…There is nothing more important than perhaps keeping the fires going." MT looked around as if a more crucial task might present itself. "We are lucky to have a woman of your talents…tasked with something this important. You and Merek: our lives are in your hands."

That evening, Merek tended the fire in the Great Room and asked the women if they had ever heard of emeralds. A fine gemstone the color of the Mallards that had landed that day. (He had learned of them from a cook with a wealthy patron who insisted on perfectly cylindrical and evenly baked breadsticks. He had had to bring the peel out of the oven several times so she could check that her dough held its shape. Merek ignored the bruises on her cheeks and the way her hands shook when she checked.) "The emerald endows the owner with the ability to foresee the future when the stone is placed under the tongue," he said as he jostled the fire. "They reveal the truth, cure cholera, and some even say they protect against evil spells."

Gertrude shuffled in her seat. "You set our minds ablaze, Baker."

His stories seemed to be the only marker of time, and night after night, Merek drew out the hunt for Prester John, revealing it in chapters to give them a sense of progress and accomplishment even if it was just the meanderings of wretched sailors. He stood very erect in front of them, his right hand clasping the stub of his left arm and Gertrude thought he looked very refined: it was the way a gentleman would stand. Even more so when he stood with his arms behind his back like a confident bishop. *His eyes, though*, she thought. They held a sadness that was tender and resigned, as if behind every story there was another one too sad to tell. The facts were the facts and telling those, his eyes were clear, but as soon as he started his fanciful tales, his eyes grew wistful and she could tell that he was shielding his listeners, sifting out the heartbreak. She wanted to cup his cheek in her hand.

~ * ~ * ~ * ~

It rained for six weeks.

The children grew anxious that there were no birds in the sky and wondered where they had gone. Four women who were determined to go to the chapel turned back when one slid half-way down the hill in the mud. MT had ordered Jacob to remain in the manor despite his worry over the queendoms. He clung to the windowsill looking uphill though the coneygarth was not visible. The incessant noise of the rain, like a scratching on the roof, grated on everyone's nerves and just when they managed to ignore it a huge clap of thunder rattled them again. MT found a young woman in the corner with her hands over her ears, crying. An old ewe that couldn't handle the changes died in the night and Claudia taught Percy (without letting on to the others that he didn't know) to butcher and skin it. Some of the mutton was set aside for the dogs. The women were pleased with the change in diet, so Claudia didn't tell them it was a sign that even the animals were becoming desperate. The gloom made some of the women sleepy and lethargic and those who turned their worry into constant movement bickered with them for not pulling their weight.

MT was one of those constantly on the move. She entered all the rooms, checking the window sashes for signs of dampness, listening to the sound of the water; like a river at the south end roof; a creek over the back door; a stream at the side wall; intermittent splashing in the courtyard. Different than yesterday? A new sound of leakage? She made the rounds: river, creek, stream, splashes; river, creek, stream. She peered into the pantry and calculated again, then paced the hallways until one afternoon she stood in front of the door at the far side of the house that she had closed off with a heavy sideboard when they first arrived. It was the only place not filled with the staff's anxiety and she needed to hear the rain there, so MT put her shoulder into it and moved the sideboard, opened the door. She paced through the empty section of the manor house comprised of a large, sunny salon, with connected bedrooms that ran the length of the manor. The floors were dry. The walls showed no snaking line of leaks. Fluted columns, patterned floors, a huge hearth topped by an enormous, carved mantlepiece. Windows with perfect mullions and stained-glass sigils above carved wainscoting. The bedrooms were empty except for narrow beds that had been stripped of their mattresses. Room by room, she walked the long expanse of wood floors.

The finery of the salon seemed particularly obscene in the face of their pending starvation. This could not happen to them. With thirty people to feed, they could last maybe another two months by slaughtering the livestock including the rabbits, she calculated. But then what? No one had seen rain last this long so no one could predict when it would end. Five months? She raised her eyes to think, and she marveled at the high windows. All with southern exposures, these were the sunniest rooms in the building. Weak light but still, more glass than anywhere in the manor. The destruction of their garden would make her community untenable, she knew, but she was stuck. Inside, dry sun but no plants, no soil. Outside, soil sodden from the battering rain. If only one could be with the other.

MT looked around the room. Why not bring the garden inside? Because it would damage the floors. Rot them out entirely, she knew. Agreeing to that would mark her once and for all as no member of the gentry. But this was no time to protect the farce. Pot the plants and put them here. Not just pots, she thought, warming to her idea and pacing through the room. Troughs, bins, buckets, anything that could hold soil. Excited, she walked through the hall that connected the pantries and kitchen, through the entryway and back to the salon and the unused bedrooms on the other side. If the vegetables grew the rabbits would live and chickens might lay, and her community might be saved. Life or death hung on the success of pole beans and carrots.

MT summoned Percy, who was spending his days in the outbuildings trying to soothe his livestock while he dreamed of a life with Claudia. MT called on Merek because he was strong and good with an axe. Claudia took a moment from her brood of children and gathered the strongest young women as well as Jacob, and they collected buckets, barrels and troughs to put in the rooms. The first task, MT said, was to gather the vegetables that had already been saved and were being stored in damp cloth. They took care not to break the roots or stalks though they had to throw much of it into the feed bucket because it was too damaged by the rain. When they saw how little was left, they tried not to panic. They threw on cloaks and took turns rushing outside to dig up anything they could find.

Merek, however, alerted her to another problem: the first bucket of soil brought in from the raised beds was sodden and unusable. Water dripped from the bucket onto the floor. She waved him out of the room, and they went back outside to stand under the eaves and consider. Percy joined them. By the time they broke for a brief lunch of pulped fruit, they had a system. Small holes in the lower sides of the buckets. Buckets set on stones above the walkway to pour off the worst of the water, then taken to the laundry and emptied into sacks. The sacks would be squeezed between a wooden press and the water would pour onto the slanted stone floor to drain outside. Sacks would be emptied into hand carts and taken to the bakery where the soil, wet but not sodden, would be raked out in troughs and allowed to warm slightly by a fire they decided to afford. Back into the hand carts and off to the sunny rooms where it was shoveled into low barrels.

MT told the little sentry to ring the bell once anytime there was a momentary break in the rain so they could run out to fill buckets and collect battered plants. When she returned to the salon, she protested.

"No, no," MT said, wiping her hands on an apron she had borrowed from the kitchen. "These barrels from the brewery are too deep. It will require too much soil, too much work. Cut them in half and just put the top ring right on the floor. Next to the bottom of the barrel. In fact, cut them into three pieces. Two without bottoms and one with."

"Milady," Claudia protested, then lowered her voice. "You will ruin the floor."

"My floor," MT reminded her.

"The manor house floor of the barony," Claudia whispered. "Within the dukedom. Ultimately a gift given by the king."

"Who will no doubt prefer live subjects to pretty floors," MT said loud enough for others to hear. "And if not, I shall remind him of God's priorities." The fact that the plan lacked grandeur, she realized with a sly smile, was a bonus because it damaged precious woodwork she had spent her former life tending. It flew in the face of the beds and salons that the common folk never enjoyed. A rebellion. "Use the pillars as support for the beans," she ordered, smiling at the plan to run ordinary vegetation up the grand columns with their carved wooden birds, harps, and grapes.

At first the workers were sloppy, tramping mud across the floor, grinding it in with their boot heels. Soon, however, pride in their work made the rows straight and the soil contained within the beds, the buckets moved in the sun to best effect. Every day, the whole staff came into the rooms to marvel at the progress, noting the new shoots, the blossoms, the vines. A peasant's garden in a gentry's salon, they laughed.

Merek saw MT's delight. "So, we'll have a fire laid here all the time, in the…what are we calling it?"

MT hadn't considered. "The Window Room? The Conclave? The Garden Room?"

"Garden Room."

When MT was told of dinner and called the day's work to a

halt, the household was filled with a lightness it hadn't known it could retrieve. It might have been the result of working all day in the little sunshine that snuck through the rain, or the prospect of a solution to their problems. Jacob skipped down the halls without a shirt on, which delighted the young women, and MT took note of which women were most enchanted. She surreptitiously followed him down the hall, peeking around corners. The farther the servants walked away from MT the more boisterous they became, with Jacob included in their reverie. She sat at the head table alone, again.

Gertrude delivered MT's dinner herself and glared at the bejeweled cap as she set down the bowl of thin soup. No gentry would allow the floors to be ruined which meant that the baroness was not a woman of any sort of importance at all. They called her Lady Hope. She considered her Lady Charade. But something had to be done and this crazy plan, Gertrude though, shaking her head. At least the baroness wasn't thinking only of herself.

CHAPTER THIRTEEN

At night between the first and second sleep, Merek rose to groggily bank the fire in the kitchen and check on the smoker where the dogs slept in a semi-circle, basking in the warmth and aroma. MT wandered the halls with a smudge stick, drawing patterns with the smoke as if a solution would write itself. Returning to the library, MT caught a glimpse of herself in the mirror on the door and thought the white cap looked like a cluster of votive candles.

The next morning, MT surveyed the woodpile and was concerned. How long would it last? How long would it rain? They should consolidate. She considered having the children play in her library but worried about the gold and the need she and Claudia had to plot in private. She ordered that they stop lighting a fire in the library, which surprised the staff that once again she wasn't placing herself above them, but it frightened them: for a royal to scrimp meant they were in very dire straits.

In the morning, she found a small cluster of women praying together and several of the young girls had been crying.

Then it was clear that even five fires – the kitchen, the smoker, the nursery, the Great Room, and the Garden Room – were too many. Consolidation. Merek suggested that they close down the smoker and hang the meat in the Garden Room.

"Yes. And bring the children to the central hearth," MT said, though she knew Claudia would complain that the babies needed quiet for naps. "So, we will heat only the kitchen, the Great Room where most will congregate and the Garden Room for the sake of the plants."

"I could go out to chop more," Merek said tentatively.

"No. It won't do to have you fall ill and we can't dry the wood anyway. Assess the stockpile and report to me again."

The following afternoon MT was grateful that everyone was busy and out of bed though Merek had almost reached an unidentified, shrill whine he was investigating when they realized that it was the sound of wood giving way. The entire roof of the servants' quarters collapsed under the weight of the pooling rain. All the bedding and carefully constructed ticking was suddenly buried under a layer of planking and shingles. The seamstresses and maids who ran there stood in each other's arms watching the sheets and blankets darken with water and soak up the mud from the roof.

They called out to anyone trapped, sent a girl to count heads and were relieved when everyone was accounted for.

Merek put a rope around the orphan boy because he was the lightest among them and he was sent out to retrieve what linens he could from the rubble.

Arriving at the scene, MT sensed their despair, and it made her bark orders. "Careful not to tear them if possible. How does the floor seem, Merek?"

"Sturdy enough for the light ones, milady."

"You two, in," she said. "Don't pull the cloth from under the planks: you'll rip them. Move the planks. Careful of your hands. You two follow behind and collect the cloth. Only two in at a time. We'll deal with the ticking when we can. Bring them here and wring them out into buckets. You know what to do. Courage now. We have courage for this, too. Merek, with me."

An older woman comforted the girls. "Don't worry. Milady knows what to do. Take them to the laundry."

MT and Merek paced toward the bakery to inspect the woodpile. "Will trials never cease," she muttered to him under her breath. But they did have courage for this, she realized. After the months of her bear-like plodding and fearful hiding under the pelt as far north as she could walk, she had the courage for this, as well. She had grown into her position.

"They'll need to sleep in the Great Room: there's nowhere else," she said. "And now we need a fire big enough to dry bedding." They stared at the woodpile. "How does it look, Merek?"

"We have slowed usage, that's true. Still not enough for five months, though."

"I will not let us die," MT said emphatically as she paced

back and forth in front of the woodpile. "We have brought the outside inside so what else can the inside do for us? Could Gertrude cook at the central hearth in the Great Room?"

"Oh, milady…" Merek shook his head as a warning.

She grunted. *I shudder to think of the diatribe. She already thinks we live on the edge of savagery.*

"What if…" MT said, "what if she believed that the central hearth was a step up, an advancement?"

"Or the kitchen was made something else, unfit for cooking, and it drove her out?" Merek hated to plot against Gertrude, but this was too important. "Like, an abattoir."

"Very good! Butchering animals in the kitchen. Work with Claudia and Percy. Roast a piglet or a lamb on a spit in the Great Room. I'll move all the best candlesticks from the library. It will be better for her not to be separated from the rest of us anyway."

Merek smiled at her, bowed his head and set to his task building Gertrude a spit.

MT sequestered herself in the library, though there was no fire there. She could monitor the progress from the sounds that carried down the hall. As she predicted, Gertrude pounded on the door to register her complaint, but MT didn't allow her in and said nothing. Then she heard the sound of the pot hook and the andirons being moved, the jostling pots and ladles, the spit being assembled. The short squeal of the piglet being slaughtered, more shrieking from Gertrude, and finally the smell of roasting meat. When she emerged, she acted surprised.

"Oh Gertrude, what a great idea! To join us! To bathe us in

the aroma of your fine cooking. To show the young ones how it's done." She turned to the children sitting in rapt attention at the delicious meat. "Now pay attention, children. You are blessed to have such a skilled cook to learn from." She stepped forward and grasped Gertrude's elbow. "Warmth, camaraderie, and a chef: what more could one ask for?" MT looked over the room at the tired faces of the women as the firelight bounced off her cap. "Except perhaps a song. Who can lead us in something lively?"

Two girls jumped up to sing a ditty. An older woman began a hymn until the room was filled with song. The babies settled and slept. The basting juice slid off the pig and sizzled on the hearth.

MT walked to the far end of the Great Room where it joined the hallway to the Garden Room. Claudia, her arm draped with a heavy load of clean, wet linens, came to her side.

"How long will this rain last?" Claudia asked under her breath.

"However long," MT said resolutely as she looked out at the women, "we will outlast it."

Claudia turned to her, impressed, and curtsied deeply without irony. "Milady."

They decided: children in the right corner nearest the fire. Gertrude's cooking table to the left. Ticking straw fluffed and turned over to dry four feet from the hearth to give Gertrude and her scullery girl room to work. Dried ticking given first to the oldest women. Bedding moved to the far wall during the day and laid out at night. The seamstresses brought the drying racks up from the laundry, unhappy that they had been forbidden from building even one fire under a washing kettle and so the bedding was not as clean as they would have liked. Steam rose from the linens as they dried.

"Our sheets will smell like pork," one girl said.

"Better that than rabbit…"

"Again!" the two girls said in unison.

The seamstresses got busy repairing or replacing the bedding that had been lost and Claudia had the children run relay races down the halls to exhaust them. MT sat near the fire at night in the biggest chair in the hall and clapped as they sang and danced but couldn't help her constant calculations. The smoker held nine fish and four ducks. New friendships had been formed. The children looked oblivious, as they should.

The rain affected everything: their dancing was frenzied to match the patter; the children ran up and down the rows of vegetables as if animated by a crazed drumbeat. They pleaded with Gertrude to stop making soup: while it was warm and comforting, putting liquid inside while trying to avoid the liquid outside was too demoralizing. And without bread – even old bread, dry bread, a crust of bread – everything seemed made of mush. Boiled fruit, mashed root vegetables, their own feet, their beds at night. Gertrude switched to daily roasting, even if it was rabbit.

The question on everyone's mind was "when will it stop" though the lack of an answer was so disconcerting that even the children stopped asking it out loud.

"Tell us a story, Baker," Gertrude said that evening.

Merek began with stories of sailors swept into the ocean by huge waves, and with wild gestures and his glowing poker, he lunged toward the children. Rain dissolved the walls of Prester John's castle, he said, and the two-headed horses got lost. Claudia scowled at him, and when he saw the children huddling closer together and Jacob sitting wide-eyed, he cleared his throat and began again. Stories of rain made of liquid gold that coated the sheep in the field and made their spun wool into gold thread without effort; rain that pooled at the base of a willow tree so that the faeries could have their annual diving contest from the branches.

The next night, Merek told them that the rain had opened a wider world to the fish and their queen – a stately female whose scales sparkled and who had tendrils from her head that glistened red and blue. The queen gleefully sent them on expeditions into flooded places where no fish had ever gone and they marveled at the milking stools and gardening tools they had never seen, swimming into chapels and sitting on their tails in the pews to give thanks for the rain that changed their world. They swam around headstones that were submerged and gates that were pointless. Even into cottages! Unfortunately, he said as he re-set a log on the fire, the princess of the fish got caught in the weave of a loom and it took two days to free her with all the fish nibbling at the thread and her mother the queen whispering soothing words to keep her from thrashing around and becoming more tangled.

By the end of the week, Merek told of the fish swimming along mantles and marveling at candlesticks just as the fish-king returned. There was a great celebration, he said, until the fish-king, with sweeping speeches and puffed-out cheeks, convinced the fish that they ruled the whole world. The queen knew better, of course, Merek whispered to the children, but was unable to stop the fish-king in an ill-fated attempt to conquer the birds. "Not advisable," he said, leaning into them, and they nodded their little heads in agreement. During the battle, the fish queen led her school safely back into the river, but the king and his knights were trapped in a puddle under a willow tree and when the tide receded they were a delicious meal for a falcon and her chicks.

As Merek continued, Claudia knelt on one knee beside MT's chair to whisper. "We have no more fabric, or even thread, milady. I'm concerned that without projects, the women will become even more distraught."

MT nodded but said nothing to Claudia. "Baker, a fine story," MT said to the group. "The queen leads them where all is right with the world again. On that note, time for bed, children."

MT slipped away and though they had fixed a bed with a screen around it for her in the Great Room nearest the fire, she went into the cold library. Opening the baroness's closet, she first double-checked for extra blankets or quilts though she had brought those out when the roof collapsed. It was wrong for a woman to have so many dresses when others had nothing to sleep on, she thought. She struggled again with keeping up the pretext or doing what was right.

In the past she had been focused on her desire to lead but hadn't realized how exhausting it was to be relentlessly responsible. They were counting on her, though. What was here that could help? The linings, she thought. She could detach the linings from the dresses and if she straightened them out Claudia might be able to pass them off as a newly discovered bolt of cloth. By candlelight she picked at the stitching and Claudia found her there in the morning asleep with two spools of thread and twelve yards of fabric. No lace, fur, gold thread or brocade: Claudia was heartened by MT's understanding of the subterfuge.

They devised a new system to keep towels, blankets and themselves warm and dry: anyone returning from outdoor chores stripped off their clothing behind a screen by the fire and warmed themselves in whatever spare underclothes were available and the blankets that weren't already on beds against the wall. Their clothes were hung on a hook, twisted repeatedly to wring the water into a pan below, shaken out and left until the steam stopped rising from them. Gertrude thought that all of these hanging towels and damp clothing made the Great Room look shabby but relented when Merek stood beside her to tousle his hair and wrap a warm towel around his neck.

As they worked, the staff quietly debated their understanding of the baroness. They had previously approached MT as if she was a dog that hadn't shown its teeth: wary of her as they kept track of her strange and overly familiar behavior. But now that so many of her plans had turned out right, even if MT was not a baroness, she could be respected, couldn't she? And with the rain making the outside world impassable, it wouldn't pay to get on her wrong side and be tossed out. Their real enemy was the rain.

When yet another Monday of the deluge dawned and the staff glumly set to tasks, MT smiled broadly with a new idea.

"Bring the bearskin from my chambers," she ordered. "And drag the biggest chair from the high table over here." She ordered another chair broken into parts and had the legs attached to the side of the high-back chair. Covering it with the bearskin, it was as if the animal had entered the room, and the maids stepped back a bit in awe. MT smiled at their stunned faces, and called over a young, thin maid who was keeping her cold hands under her armpits. "In you go," she ordered, and the young woman hesitated, then tucked her legs under her and disappeared into the cavern of the bear-like chair. MT chuckled and clapped her hands together. When they peered into it a few minutes later, the maid was fast asleep.

CHAPTER FOURTEEN

In the library, Claudia was helping MT out of her dress which had been soaked by her early-morning inspection of the livestock and the eaves. With her head still in the folds of the skirt, MT was suggesting that they build an awning from the front door to the side stalls right and left, but their musings were interrupted by the unexpected sound of someone throwing rocks at the roof. MT and Claudia went to the window, then both leaned backward in disbelief.

Hailstones as big as goose eggs were pelting the manor house, bouncing off the cobblestones. Two of the ducks in the courtyard were struck and killed instantly. MT heard the housemaids shrieking as they ran to the windows. Shortly, a maid came in holding an injured arm followed by another reporting that fish were being struck in the pond and dying.

The chickens weren't laying and were now being displaced by the ducks so no eggs. Now their fish were being killed by the hail. MT thought of her inventory of the thin larder: they hadn't been in the manor house long enough to put up a surplus of dried or pickled anything. Barrels that were generally filled with apples had been emptied by scavengers months ago, she had seen while standing on a stool to peer over the rim and while they gathered what they could it was nearly empty. She had thought she would request that someone find or make a butter churn, though there hadn't been milk for two days. If the hens stopped laying and the cow was too distraught for milk they would have to butcher some of the young sheep.

"We can't leave the chickens outside to be killed by hail. So…somewhere inside," MT said. "Chickens are in the outbuildings and the courtyard but it's more building than they need. So, chickens into the laundry…If the ceiling is still tight enough after the roof collapsed above it."

"The laundry?" Claudia challenged.

"I won't let us starve to protect a ruse! We need food. Chickens more than clean clothes. And fish. That's an idea. Take out the linen linings from the laundry tubs and make them fishponds. Chicken and fish farms in the laundry. Sheep in the outbuildings. No pigs in the house, though. I draw the line there."

"Glad to hear there is one, somewhere!" Claudia said.

Gertrude the cook entered the library and curtsied. "Milady, the hail has stripped the fruit trees."

"Then the minute it's safe, send the girls out to collect it all. Harvest everything on the trees, ripe or not."

It hailed for the rest of the day until the courtyard was carpeted ankle deep in hard, round hailstones. During a break between the hail and the resumption of the rain, Percy and several of the girls moved the nesting boxes into the laundry.

After another week of pounding rain, MT grew concerned for Jacob who wouldn't be separated from his rabbits any longer and had returned to his fortress a week ago. At sunset, she grabbed her cloak and boots and set out to find him. She waved away any attempt to accompany her, knowing that it would reveal the secret tryst of the baroness which would jeopardize Jacob. But there was a longing to see him that she hadn't experienced and an illogical desire to keep their secret. Her dear Jacob, she thought as she struggled to climb the sodden hill in the near-vertical rain.

She couldn't raise a response when she pounded on the lodge door, which doubled her worry. She paced out toward the ribbons that were now soaked and limp and saw him trapping rabbits and stuffing them into baskets arranged on a cart. She ran toward him, holding her hood.

Over the deluge, he shouted to her of his tragedies: all rabbits in the pillow mound of Matilda had been drowned, he wailed, and other coneygarths were probably flooded like the rest of the countryside. She stepped toward him and took his hand.

"Which queendom is next?" she asked him, and he gestured to Eleanor of Aquitaine's pillow mound. They each took one handle of the cart and pushed against the wind. She had no experience with rabbits, so she held the baskets, snapping the lid down after they were inserted. But there were more rabbits than baskets, and the cart was already overfilled.

MT gestured to the lodge, but he protested that there were two more rabbit colonies to save. "We'll come back, Jacob," she shouted, wiping the rain off her face. "Let's save these and come back." He and MT struggled in the mud to get the cart to the lodge.

Just inside the door, MT stood motionless. More than a hundred rabbits covered the warren floor. "Upstairs," Jacob said, and they carried the baskets into the living quarters where he emptied the baskets onto the floor. MT surveyed the room. There were already thirty rabbits on the floor, the bed, under the table, many in little dresses, most with beaded necklaces. He had been rescuing them since the hailstorm. Jacob rushed past her to bring more baskets from the cart. As he stacked the empty baskets and got ready to go back into the rain, she grabbed his arm. He was soaked to the skin and shivering.

"...but the colony of...," he said weakly and gestured to the door.

"I command you to stay," she said with chagrin. When he bowed in sad submission she dropped her hand from his arm. She took off her cape and turned to stoke the fire but was surprised by a roaring sound they couldn't place. Jacob cocked his head and seized a rough-hewn ladder that he rammed into a trap door in the ceiling. The two of them clambered up onto the parapet where MT, wrapping her cape around her again and pulling her hood up, was surprised by the vista.

She could see the entire barony from there, though the road she had taken to the house was underwater, the farm was flooded, the river had doubled in width and fields were submerged. She could even see the hillock, like a tiny island, where the prisoners were being held in their tent. How were they surviving in the rain? A thin column of smoke rose from the apex of the tent, and she saw that horses were tethered nearby but she wondered about how they were getting food. Just then the roaring increased, the trees shook and some toppled as a wall of water poured through the valley, upending the horses, pulling the tent up by its stakes and sweeping it into the river. She faintly heard men screaming, then silence, as all were washed away, the tent like a rag being balled-up as it was carried out of sight.

She grabbed Jacob's forearm and stood close to him. He shook his head, looked down, shook his head again.

"Like the colony of Matilda," he said sadly.

"Yes, my dear one. Like the colony of Matilda."

Water turned the forest that separated the barony from the village into a fern fringe on a pond. Only the peak of the chapel and the eaves of the hayloft on the farm remained above the water.

The rain increased in intensity.

She took his hand and led him back inside, as he was shaking with the cold, and had him sit on a chair to take off his wet shirt.

She stoked the fire and put on broth, warmed a towel and, shuffling carefully through the writhing carpet of rabbits, dried his hair and his shoulders, while he put his face in his hands and cried. She had never touched a man with such tenderness. Never tended to a man, and she squeezed the water out of his hair, wrung the rain out of his shirt as if she was a different woman, more so than even her ruse of the baroness. She had always wanted to tend to people, but she had never imagined that would involve a man. Especially a sweet boy-man like Jacob. She gently swept the rabbits from the bed and brought the blanket to him, guided him by the elbow to standing and wrapped it around his waist.

"Take your wet pants off now, Jacob, and I'll dry them at the hearth."

"Is it time for my baroness to ride me?" He clutched the blanket but slid the cap from her head.

MT had no idea what to say. Or to do.

She and Jacob stayed in bed as the rain pelted down for another night and day, MT astonished by the flush that ran through her body now, at the tension and climax, and especially at the tender attention of someone who actually desired her body – long ridiculed and privately loathed. As a child, she had never played or indulged in silly make-believe. As a woman, she had never had a lover. A sweet, tender lover.

MT had resolved, and Jacob had agreed that she would return to the manor house at noon even if there wasn't a break in the rain. There was almost nothing left to eat in the lodge so staying was not an option, and she knew that Claudia and the household would be worried about her, even though she had told them she was checking on the warrener. She should return but she didn't want to leave Jacob behind, and Jacob did not want to leave his bunnies behind.

"We'll bring them with us, then," she said, rising and dressing clumsily, unaccustomed to her nudity.

"To the house? The big house? Not the cottage?"

"No, not the cottage. To the big house. It's alright, you're safe, Jacob. The baron is long dead, and we must break all the rules to survive now."

They were soaked again by the time they reached the manor house with a cartload of rabbits, and it hurt MT to have to reassert the separation between her and Jacob, but she ordered the kitchen maids to get him dry and fed. He refused to go, though, until his rabbits were settled.

Claudia, at first relieved to see MT, put her hands on her hips at the thought of more livestock in inappropriate places.

"Where do we have a lot of barrels?" MT wondered aloud. "And pipes where they can make their home."

"You can't be serious about keeping them indoors," Claudia said.

"How is the food supply, Claudia?" MT asked.

Claudia relented. "Pipes. Maybe the brewery."

"Excellent," MT said. "Rabbits to the brewery!"

MT took Claudia aside as the kitchen maids giggled at the prospect and took Jacob by the hand to skip with him to the brewery. "Seriously, Claudia, how is the food supply?"

"The hens still aren't laying and every day we watch the garden grow slowly."

"The jail's tent was carried into the river," MT said with her voice lowered. The kitchen maids were frightened enough without thinking of a dozen dead men floating in the river. "To think of them inside." She gripped Claudia's arm, and they lowered their heads in prayer.

"We heard an enormous roar."

"That was it. Taken like cats in a bag." She should have

saved them all, initially, not just the women, MT thought. Could she have saved them? It wasn't enough. What she did was never enough.

Claudia motioned to the brewery. "We should check on them. There's no telling what they've come up with."

As they neared the brewery, they passed Gertrude who rung her hands on a towel and, though she curtsied, mumbled about the affront of animals and people under the same roof. Back to the Vikings to live in such a primitive state, she growled.

MT stopped.

"Indeed, Gertrude, these are desperate times. The great dying chose us at random but now we are tested to see what is more important than the life we are so lucky to have retained. Bring me an inventory of all foodstuffs and livestock before retiring. Please."

In the brewery, the sound of the young women's bright laughter bounced off the copper pipes until MT opened the door, and all fell silent. The maids, probably at Jacob's insistence, had opened all the rabbit baskets before having a suitable system for them, and they hopped under foot. MT sighed with consternation. She flung her hand out as if the solutions were obvious.

"Right. Open the tops of all the empty barrels and tip them on their sides. Butt ends of the barrels against the wall. We don't want them trapping themselves."

"No," Jacob said, as the rabbits hopped into the barrels and back out again. "More secret."

"Yes, of course. Turn the barrels so the opening can't be

seen from the door." She and Claudia inspected the pipes of the brewery.

"Milady, you cannot... I advise against dismantling the brewery and filling the pipes with rabbit...filth."

"Again, how is the food supply, Claudia?"

"What are we to feed rabbits, milady? We have no greens for ourselves let alone animals. You cannot..." Claudia caught herself in what sounded like impertinence.

MT gestured expansively to the room, turning the project over to Claudia who curtsied briefly and stepped in to supervise.

That evening as they gathered in the Great Room, the bear-chair was diagonal to the hearth with its back to the door looking very much like a giant animal warming itself by the fire. Upon seeing it, Jacob froze in the doorframe and a maid had to take him by the hand to approach it. But when he looked inside there were two toddlers curled up sleeping and he laughed and slapped his thigh, turned to the others, waving his arms and making shapes with his hands, approaching it and jumping back, laughing harder with every glance. His mirth delighted them all.

The next morning, Jacob brought in a large barrel from the brewery that he had cut in half horizontally and a quarter panel cut off vertically, and he set it to the right of the bear, laid rabbit pelts inside it, and covered it with a fur quilt that he had spent the night sewing.

"The Bear's friend," he said triumphantly. "A coney-cave. For the little ones."

The frivolity of a bear and a giant rabbit sitting hearthside cheered them every time they entered the room, and it did as much to sustain them as extra food. They took turns sitting in the bear-chair every day, and though it was the warmest place in the manor house, its comfort went beyond its warmth. The heavy animal and sage odor of the bear-chair became the scent of protection. Deep inside the musky tent of it, grown women felt enveloped in a mother's love again, protected by someone stronger than they were constantly asked to be. They could rest, narrowing the world to the dark pelt and a good fire. It had been MT's comfort one winter on the road where she parked the cart in a cliffside cave just outside an abandoned but food-rich village in northern Scotland. She stood at the mouth of the cave, watching the trees swaying in the distance and, entranced, started swaying with them. A bird swooped by, and she twirled with it, then jumped as it hopped into branches, and unlike any nun she had ever seen, slid across the smooth stone cave floor, throwing her arms out and dipping her head. When the fog rolled in she lit a fire at the cave lip and watched the fog obliterate the world outside. It had been her most northern point: the solace of the cave fighting with the solitude of the dales. She headed south in the spring, anxious for company.

Merek's story that night was of Baroness the Bear and her journey with Lady Coney to the land of Prester John, which, he announced with a flourish, was a tale of heroism and wisdom.

The next morning, MT folded her arms across her chest and was considering the progress in the garden room when there was a tug at her sleeve.

"A horse!" the young sentry said.

When MT, Claudia and the young boy crossed the courtyard with capes over their heads, the horse in her stall was whinnying and stomping her hooves. Climbing to the lookout, they saw a horse swimming toward their shore of the flooded valley. Claudia clambered back down to the courtyard, strained to lift the bar across the front gate and pushed the doors open. Despite the rain, she brought the horse out of its stall hoping it could stand on the hill as a beacon for the swimmer. But between the wet reins and the strength of the horse, it wrested itself free of Claudia and ran down the hill to the water's edge. Percy ran out beside Claudia to watch his horse escape.

"I'm sorry...I," she said, flummoxed.

"Get out of the rain," he told her and returned to the corral, then reemerged with a lead rope and watched from the top of the hill. The swimmer redirected itself and reached the shore near Percy's horse. The two horses stood under the trees getting acquainted until Percy whistled. His mare started up the hill, the swimmer followed, and the two horses trotted into the courtyard.

Percy smiled at the impressed look on Claudia's face.

MT left Percy and Claudia to dry and settle the new horse but when she stepped inside, a maid curtsied and beckoned her to the laundry room. The girls had left the linen linings in the wash tubs and the fish had died from the soap. They floated on the top of the water, and her flock was worse off than if she had left the fish in the pond to be killed by the hail.

Late that night in the library, MT and Claudia paced the floor, struggling with their own puzzles and frazzled by the rain but directing their anger at each other.

"I see the way you look at Jacob," Claudia challenged, fear driving her more than anger. "You're in love with him, aren't you. Mary Mother of God. That's perfect for you, isn't it? You want to be in charge of everything and so you love a simpleton, a man who has no ability to challenge you. Always the boss, aren't you?"

"Me? You wanted a child and now that you've scarred her she'll never be married and leave you. You got what you want, at her expense!"

The moment she said it, MT felt as if she wanted to retract the words like stuffing birds back into a bag. "I'm sorry. It was an accident. I…"

"No, no," Claudia said with resignation and a distance in her voice. "That's how you feel…"

"I don't, Claudia. I just…don't know how to love a man. Especially this man who is…so precious. Fragile." *Exuberant*, she thought to herself, remembering the way they had laughed with the bunnies and the little beads. The dresses. Laughter she didn't know she had in her. Laughter that had been taken from her. Delight. She had had a childhood devoid of delight. Small wonders that were easily crushed.

Perhaps that is why she had stuck it out with Simon for so long: the Abbess, seeing the little novices exploring a caterpillar, denounced it as the ruination of the garden and squished it in front of their faces. Apple blossom branches in a vase on the table had to be carried to the bloodied feet of

Jesus. Like Simon, her first Abbess stomped on delight like bugs in the chapel.

MT went to bed early and tossed in the night. The maids were looking sallow, and their energy flagged in the early afternoon. Every day it was more difficult to think of things for them to do so they didn't spend the day despondently looking out the window. There wasn't even floss for embroidery or weaving. Gertrude's collar bones could be seen through her blouse.

She was foolish to think she could do this. And it was her responsibility to find a solution. They looked to her. That's what leadership is, isn't it? Having the best idea. Devising the best plan, charting the right course. She remembered one of the Abbesses, years ago when MT was just a teen, and how the nuns talked behind the Abbess's back about all her wrong decisions, all the ways she kept them from what was right and effective. They talked about her like she was an object, or a condition, like bad weather, with no regard for her feelings. The Abbess's position exalted her but at the same time, it reduced her humanity, and with that, the nuns' compassion for her. MT had no doubt that the kitchen maids were spinning stories of her bad ideas and the fish floating in the laundry tub.

So, MT was wide awake when the alarm bell sounded, though it was a quiet ring. She threw a fur-lined cape over her nightdress and hurried down the hall. The old man and young boy who stood watch supported a muddy sack of bones that turned out to be a young woman, frail and weak with hunger, soaked to the skin and trembling with cold, with four despondent and frightened children clinging to her hem.

"Begging your forgiveness, milady," the old man said, "not waiting for your permission but the family seemed to be dying before our eyes. I've smudged them, though."

"Yes, you've done well. We'll help them into the Great Room. Stoke the fire, then wake one of the kitchen maids for hot broth."

MT pulled blankets onto the hearth and helped the woman to lie down. Claudia entered just as MT opened the woman's shawl to underdress her but on her chest lay a tiny, swaddled baby. Claudia charged forward, scooped up the baby and held it to her ear to see if it was still alive.

MT hurried to the kitchen for the broth and Percy was on her heels when they returned. MT threw open the door but stopped with her hand still on the doorknob as she surveyed the room. In the corner, Claudia was nursing the baby, both of her breasts exposed, her hair loosened, and the four children between her legs alternately suckling at her other breast. MT thought she saw a ravenous look on Claudia's face that was as hungry as the children's. There was something unhinged and obscene about it. Percy was shocked, then turned away to give Claudia privacy and with a puzzled glance back at her, left the room.

Claudia tucked her breasts away as maids flooded into the room with towels and blankets. They undressed the now unconscious woman, wrapped her in rough linen, then blankets, dried her hair, tried to wake her enough to pour broth down her throat. She was so thin her hips protruded, and MT could make out the individual bones in her arms and legs.

Claudia brought the children back to the fire and covered

their heads, helped them drink the warm broth, stripped off their rain-soaked clothes and wrapped them in blankets before putting them into the bear-chair. She asked their names, but they were too traumatized to answer, and they only occasionally stole glances at their mother. Claudia was resolved: after the children who ran from her and the children on the road that she had pretended not to see, she would not ignore these children.

The maids whispered questions to each other: who was this family and how far had they walked? How did they make it through the flood? How long since they had been without food? It had been raining for months. Looking down at her, they thought of themselves and tried to recall what old women did to get hens to lay, and they wondered about Percy's cow. They trailed off to bed, frightened and resolved to conserve their strength.

Claudia stared into the fire with two children under each arm and the baby in her lap, Daisy in a cradle. She thought about Percy but all the affection she had felt and the flirtation she had entertained drained away. A coldness settled over her. She and Percy had no future. Someday if not today, he will ask questions. Demand explanations. What man wouldn't? She couldn't trust him, not completely, could she and if there wasn't complete and absolute trust, then she couldn't risk it. Risk her children. Risk the story of the little baroness. Besides, he would want his own children, or they would inevitably be conceived, but she couldn't give him that. She couldn't bear a live child. And her heart couldn't possibly go through another death. She could be a mother, but she couldn't be a wife. When Percy returned with more wood for the fire, she looked away.

When MT returned with more blankets she found Claudia talking to the hungry children she had placed in the bear-chair.

"In the spring, we'll have pears and plums, and you can help me…"

When the last one drifted off to sleep MT took Claudia by the elbow. "They're not yours, you understand," MT said quietly.

Claudia pointedly ignored her comment.

"You have a child," MT said, suddenly suspicious.

"I lost four babies," Claudia waved her hand toward the four sleeping bundles in the bear chair, Daisy in a crib and the infant in her arms.

"But these are not them," MT said. "We will ask about their village when their mother is stronger, and we'll take the whole family back when the rain stops."

"No. I won't do it," Claudia said.

"But these do not belong to you."

Claudia bent over and pulled a blanket over one of the children's shoulders.

In the library, MT fell to her knees in front of the fire and clasped her hands, trying to pray for the hungry family, for the souls of the men washed away, for deliverance from the rain. She felt nothing and heard nothing.

In the morning, MT walked into the room to see Claudia

with Daisy and the other baby cradled in her arms, standing beside the bear-chair with the four children. Their mother's pallet was moved against the far wall, the woman dead and already in a shroud.

"Now they are mine," Claudia whispered in MT's ear, and MT shuddered.

Despite the early hour, MT summoned Merek, who carried the dead woman to the manor's graveyard while the rain sluiced down on them.

There would be no funeral, and no children at the grave. "No reason to frighten the staff or jeopardize the children further," MT said weakly, though no one had asked for an explanation. Merek dug the grave and lowered the corpse in, then MT quickly shoveled the wet soil on top without asking for assistance or delegating the task. They bowed their heads and MT prayed as much for Claudia's soul as the woman's. She hadn't killed the woman, had she? Claudia's desire hadn't driven her over the edge, had it?

"Never seen gentry handle a shovel like that" Merek said quietly.

MT did not stiffen or flinch. "The world is a very different place now," she said, and turned to leave.

Merek took the shovel from her. "Milady." *Lady Sorrow*, he thought.

When the kitchen maids straggled out of their rooms to start work and saw that the woman was gone, they turned on their heels and whispered the news to one another. Would they die like that? They were already hungry all day. The soup was barely more than water. Even big Claudia was melting away, her cheeks hollowing out and her dress hanging a bit loose on her shoulders.

The soup pot became thinner while the vegetables struggled to grow in the weak sun of the Garden Room. Percy had plenty of experience with thin soup. During a winter with arctic air that screamed across the beach throwing ice and frozen sand through the cracks of their huts, the hamlet had gathered around a pot boiling a single bone. He had stood on a stool wrapped in his mother's arms and her cape, inhaling her aroma of seaweed and salt, and watched just one bone – all they had – bob around in the roiling water. When Percy had first arrived at the manor house it pained him to throw bones to the dogs that had more meat on them than those that had fed the entire hamlet. He had gobbled his food, wide eyed at the abundance until the kennel manager touched him lightly on the arm and whispered, "no need to rush. You'll eat like this every day."

Even MT had shrunk inside her tailored clothes though not as much as the others because she had another secret.

When she first arrived at the manor, she had hidden the ham she had found with the wine in the compartment where she had found the Bible and cut slices off it late at night, savoring the delicious fat on her tongue. At those first dinners she tried not to meet the maids' eyes when she was served a generous portion of rabbit, telling herself that she was play-acting the greed of the gentry. Weekly, though, (and it took discipline to make sure it wasn't nightly) she crept into the kitchen at night, careful not to wake the maid who was to tend the fire, and she removed a large piece of rabbit from the stew pot. She stood right outside the kitchen entrance, the broth and juices dripping from her mouth and between her fingers as she ate it with her hands. The maids were perplexed by the greasy puddle they found in the morning.

On the road, long before she had arrived here, she had anxiously, voraciously sought food. Witnessing the bacchanal, she had carried her smoking sage stick and stepped over the bodies to get to the banquet table, sliding a plate out from under a young man's hand and devouring the leftovers, descending on the suckling pig until she was nauseous and then carving the rest for the road. She took loaves of bread and the plates they sat on, the cheese with the board and knife. Any pot of jam, pickles or preserved fruit, a winter's worth of oat cakes. She would have taken banquet-sized cauldrons if she had been strong enough and tall enough to lift them into her cart. She raided smoke houses and root cellars until she had an entire village's stock, then stripped gardens of everything edible, even if it took her days and filled her cart so that it was almost impossible to push. She built a fire and gorged on the food, telling herself that waste was a sin while a little voice inside reminded her that gluttony was as well. But when the cart was just light enough to be moved, she walked on and raided the next garden and larder, making large pots of boiled greens without chopping them and she spooned them into her mouth in long ribbons so that the stains on the front of her habit weren't just from a life on the road, they were all the splashes and splatters of her frenzied eating. On the road with

Simon, she was protective of her food hoard, as he was with his loot, denying each other a peek, and when his back was turned or he had gone into the woods to piss, she wrapped a bit of something into a kerchief and hid it in her bedroll so she could gnaw on it at night. She didn't accompany him into ale houses because she didn't want anyone to see how she ate, and she was (rightly) afraid of what she would do if she gained a taste for ale. When the maid had been hung and MT was discovered polishing the walls, she had actually been so distraught that she was on her knees in front of her food hoard crying and stuffing oat cakes into her mouth, just polishing while she chewed.

Now that people were starving, and everyone counted the food supply, she silently counted her private stash in the library with both fear of discovery and fear of depletion. She had half a dozen smoked fish, two rabbits, and a pound of dried apples.

Now there were four more mouths to feed and almost no food. The kitchen maids cried quietly but MT left them, looking for a quiet place to think.

CHAPTER FIFTEEN

In the morning, the windows of the Garden Room were steamed up and the air smelled beautifully of peat. Merek whispered to the maids that MT wore a garden sprite's crown, but it did little to lift their gloom. The vines were making progress, he said. Carrot tops looked healthy. He was dividing his time between the fire at the main hearth in the Great Room and the one in the Garden Room but offered MT a suggestion: if they used the main hearth just for cooking, then dampened it down, they could keep a consistent, larger fire in the Garden Room. The seamstresses and those tending the crops would be together. If they slept there they could afford to keep it warm. Crowd 30 people into the Garden Room? They would have to sleep between the vegetable beds, she protested, but it had come to this. MT stood at the head of the carrot bed and announced that from then on, they would all gather here, day and night. Keep the festivities together, she said, trying to put a happy face to it, despite the confusion on the servants' faces.

"We'll bring the bear!" Jacob shouted.

MT smiled. "Yes. With the bear."

The move became a procession with Jacob in the lead.

"Baroness," he said, gesturing to the bear-chair, and she laughed and climbed into its deep shelter, breathing deep of all the times it had protected her. The men lifted the chair, Claudia put both babies into the coney-cave and Jacob stepped like a majorette with a bit of stick, followed by the bear, the rabbit and the rest of them singing ditties and waving scarves, banging spoons on plates as they marched down the hall with all the ticking and blankets.

That evening Merek thought that MT, who was sitting in front of the fire in her black cap, looked like a bed of the best coals: steady, warm and inviting.

"Did you hear the story of the Lady of the Hearth Fire?" he asked the children. They raised their faces to him and snuggled deeper into the blankets. "Once there was a Lady of the Hearth Fire who visited a small village and decided that because all the villagers were so kind-hearted that she would cast a spell so that their fires never went out, that their fires didn't need tending in the middle of the night and so the farmers could wake up refreshed, or were able to spend that precious time between first and second sleep weaving or carving, telling stories or doing the thing that parents love best. They soon discovered that the fires they built during her visit burned to a perfect bed of coals that never cooled. In the tavern pigeons on the spit cooked crisp and beautiful in just the time it took to turn for a plate and then back to the hearth. Stews of even the toughest meat were ready before the peasant coming in from the field could even take off his boots; and the apple cobblers in their cast iron pots sent up a sweet and delicious aroma the minute after the cook put the lid on. One day, a foul tempered man who saw the worst in everything arrived in the little village and suddenly the hearth fire in the tavern started to sputter."

Listening to the story with a child on her lap, MT wondered where Simon had gone. No doubt he had found a profitable little corner of the world in which to hide. They had received no visitors after the poor woman who died. Nothing arrived from the outside world, and no one braved the rain to bring prisoners or threats. She worried about how to feed everyone, but at least there were no attacks from outsiders.

Merek lowered his voice. "Being a kind-hearted person, however, the tavern keeper gave him a seat right in front of the fire and a large mug of her best ale. He fell asleep there and by the morning the Lady of the Hearth Fire had done her work: he awoke with a heart that had been warmed and was so soft that he became the kindest of them all. Even joy brought tears to his eyes, as a heart will always leak through the eyes when it melts."

The next day, struggling to find a way to keep them all from despair, Claudia decided that it would be good use of the rain to wash their clothing. She asked Percy to put a clothesline on a pulley running diagonally across the courtyard. She ordered Merek to build an extra-large fire in the garden room then banished the men to another part of the manor. One by one dresses were attached to the line, and it seemed that they skipped their way out into the rain. A toddler's little green shift hopped out. A big woman's embroidered blouse. A beet-red dress got dripping wet and when Claudia pulled on the line to make them shake off the water it seemed that they were dancing. The maids laughed and clapped, and a woman sang a jig to keep rhythm to Claudia's dancing clothes. A maid predicted that Merek would spin a story of a queen's procession and an inaugural ball.

"Closest we'll ever come!" one maid said.

MT listened to them indulgently, warmed by their good cheer.

"Look at Jacob!" a maid said.

MT scurried to the window. Jacob had stripped to his own underclothes, put his clothing on a rake and he danced it among the women's clothes, bowing to each dress in introduction, sidling the rake up to it, becoming entwined, then twirling the two sets of clothes. The water spun off them like crystals. He put his head above the collar of the red dress and shimmied suggestively toward his clothes on the rake. A sleeve clinging to his arm held the cuff of a blouse and they raised the arms in triumph. He moved to the toddler's shift and bobbing his head like a child had his own clothes bow and spin in a circle. Claudia chortled and danced the line while the maids clapped in time.

"Come in and get dry," Claudia ordered the warrener, and she helped him wring out his clothing, wrap in a blanket, and, oblivious to the near-naked women around him, sit in the bear-chair by the fire.

A few days later, they brought the chickens and ducks from

the cold laundry into the Garden Room and put nesting boxes on the shelves of an ornate, inlaid sideboard whose doors had been torn off by thieves. The chickens, inspired by the strutting ducks as well as the sunshine and warmth, started laying the next morning. Doves lined the windowsills under the eaves, and Gertrude insisted that at least a few be caught and smoked in the fireplace. The hunting dogs who had been content around the smoker traded it for the company of happy people and curled up on the floor of the Garden Room. The fighting dogs, dedicated to protecting Jacob, sat in the hallway outside the Garden Room whenever he was there or sat sentry outside the brewery when he tended the rabbits.

MT had one of the children crawl onto her lap and she used the reflected light from her cap to taunt the cat. Merek told a story of children who lived safe and sheltered behind a waterfall where fairies brought them eggs and berries to eat and wove them beautiful clothes that could fly. He carved children's toys while sitting beside a maid who used scrap cloth to make balls that the children could roll among the vegetable beds. Claudia sat far away from Percy, with Daisy and the orphan baby on her lap, and the four other children gathered around her. Daisy pulled herself up to stand for the first time. By the end of the week, she could bounce up and down on her feet.

Jacob, even more handsome in the firelight, made a beaded necklace for the bear and danced Julia the Flop-Eared in front of the fire while a girl sewed the rabbit a little cape, then a fabric crown, made her a staff with a tiny vine and a scepter with a carrot that Percy intricately carved. Jacob and the children followed Julia on the floor as she hopped in her coronation procession, and everyone applauded her ascension to a fabric throne, then broke into cheers when she quickly nibbled the carrot until it was gone, a rebellion against the royals.

They planted sage, of course, and MT stroked it like another would a dog's ear. The courgettes snaked along the floor thicker on the vine every day.

After much cajoling by the seamstresses, Claudia let down her long blonde hair and the seamstresses took turns combing and trying to braid it into a complex pattern of multiple tiers. They pulled her hair until she protested, then started again, modified the pattern but it sat lop-sided on her head. They re-braided it poorly, took it out, changed strategy and MT was struck by how good-natured Claudia was. Claudia wondered why she would want to go off alone with her children and leave all these people behind.

The staff of the manor began to see the rain as just another condition of life, no longer odd or frightening though it had gone on for two months now. The vegetables were thriving. They melted down some of the candles and applied them to three capes and hoods as protection against the rain so they could take turns walking across the courtyard, out to the fishponds, to clean the drainage troughs or repair leaks. Still, at some point every day they leaned on their broom or shovel or pulled a towel through their fingers while watching a rain more relentless than they had even heard about from the Bible.

And they recalibrated their feelings about the baroness. Whoever she was, and wherever she was from, she was saving them, again, but late at night their whispers started with the same phrase: "I've never seen a lady do that…"

MT calculated that the rabbits and chickens might now survive but there was still the question of the cow, sheep and horses. When they first arrived at the manor house, Percy drove them out into the garden where they grazed briefly and then trotted back into their shelters. Soon it was muddy and barren and the feed that Percy had brought with him was running out. Claudia led the horses in circles with a lunge line in the courtyard when she saw that they were becoming jumpy and irritable from boredom. Even though it was raining, the mares seemed happier to stretch their legs and get a brush and a rub-down afterward, and Percy was happy to stand with Claudia, inhaling the musk of a horse. A maid taught Percy to massage the frightened cow's udder until it let down its milk, so they soon had a little butter.

The sheep were the most difficult to please, though. There were too many of them for such a small outbuilding and they shuffled around and bleated like cranky babies, losing weight for lack of fresh grass. Percy and Merek removed partitions until they could stand almost single file around half the perimeter of the courtyard, but they knew more had to be done. The sheep needed to graze. Percy and Merek went out to a large tree in the pasture to see if they could find shelter from the rain under its boughs, but the water was deep around the trunk and would make them as sick as the standing water in his barn. Besides, the sheep would be very difficult to move now, since there hadn't been even a five-minute break in the rain for days and sheep were too simple-minded to know what was good for them.

"Could we bring it to them?" Percy asked tentatively. "Cut the grass and bring it? Claudia might know. I worry that it might rot. The mold would be very dangerous for them."

Merek threw his shoulders back. "Then we can dry it," he offered. "Hang it in the garden room." He wasn't a baker, but his fires were now essential for the community's well-being. First the soil, perhaps now the livestock feed. "Or cut it and spread it on racks to dry."

Percy took to the plan and recovered the sickle from the shed to cut grass each day, hauled it inside, cut the grass into small pieces and laid it out on drying racks. It wasn't perfect, but it was welcomed by the livestock.

Soon there were little celebrations: the first time all of the chickens and ducks laid on the same day, MT hid the eggs in the Garden Room for the children to find. They tentatively plucked the first vegetables from their inside garden, but when there was enough food for a saint's day they celebrated with ribbons around the only pole not supporting a bean crop and they ate hot baked apples and a chunky stew of vegetables and, of course, rabbit.

During the festivities, Claudia handed the babies to a maid and crouched down beside MT's chair. Claudia's width obscured MT from the others.

"You are brilliant at this," she said, and MT turned to her quizzically. "At building a community. This really is what you were born to do and I'm sorry to have tried to dissuade you. But this is not it. This is not yet your community. Help them with this last endeavor: help them flee the pending danger."

MT looked down at her boots, then nodded with resignation. "Rucksacks," she said. She held Claudia's hand for a moment and then called out. "Merek, have you a story of brave travelers?"

"Milady, Marco Polo has been dead for three decades now but I'm happy to tell you stories I've heard from his book, *The Marvels of the World*."

In the morning MT and Claudia ventured out to the back stables and broke into the tack room, one of the few that hadn't been ransacked. They saved tack and saddles for the two horses just in case they needed to ride but concentrated on preparations for wagons. They looked at each other warily and Claudia ordered that they be collected in two bunches, all together, easily scooped up for a quick get-away. All the remaining tack was gathered to make straps for rucksacks and binding for supplies. MT started to gather some of it in her arms and Claudia slapped the leather to the floor.

"Apparently you will never learn that the gentry do not carry things."

MT sighed with exasperation. "I used to resent them their leisure and now I resent them enforcing mine. Can you carry all of that?"

Claudia crouched down and heaved the tack in two batches onto each shoulder. "Pull up my hood," she told MT and then she rose smoothly.

"You are quite something, my friend," MT said, shaking

her head. "This would have been impossible without you. We'd be in shackles or dead from hunger, you know."

Claudia smiled down at her.

MT continued. "What am I to do now? Walk imperiously beside you with my hands free?" They stepped out into the rain.

"Enjoy it while you can. Your privilege ends at the edge of the barony."

MT grunted. "We could send Merek to harvest rushes by the river's edge. Weave them into basket rucksacks."

"Now that's what you're good at: giving orders. Edge of the barony, don't forget," she said with a sly smile.

The women sat by the fire in the Garden Room and abandoned embroidery to sew sacks, blanket covers, and sheaths for the larger knives, while others wove flat-back baskets for rucksacks. Percy, Merek and the old man carved walking sticks, "with sharp and lethal ends please," MT had whispered to them. "One for each of us." Jacob was told to harvest rabbits and create water botas from rabbit hide. Merek fired up the smoker again to cure as much meat as they could. Questions were met with false light-heartedness about selling the items in the market when the rain stopped.

"What about the children?" MT asked quietly. Claudia was adamant, remembering the vulnerable children she had seen on the road.

"Each should have a bit of what it takes. Water, warm blanket, dried meat and fruit."

Claudia turned away from the memory and gathered her

children closer that night but couldn't shake the longing to return to every child she hadn't helped.

MT called out to Merek. "Baker, tell us more of this Italian, Polo."

~ * ~ * ~ * ~

They had grown so accustomed to the roaring sound of the rain that when it stopped in the middle of the night, MT sat bolt upright in her bed. That woke Claudia, who immediately dashed to the side of her babies' cradle and only when she was sure all the children were breathing on their pallets did she turn to the window.

It was as surprising as the hail: a full moon glinting on draining rivulets in the courtyard, and sheep who had finally budged from under the roofs of the outbuildings now wandering across the flagstones.

MT breathed a sigh of relief. If this wasn't just a break in the relentless rain, she had gotten her clan through it. They had lost several chickens, one of the sheep was probably too sick with rain rot to make it, and there was no doubt that quite a number of rabbits had drowned, but her staff, her little congregation had all made it. Except for the woman they hung by the road, she reminded herself. And the starving woman who died. (Was she killed, she wondered?) She said a prayer for the men who had drowned in the tent and briefly wondered whether the sheriff had drowned with the prisoners and posse. She dressed hurriedly. The farm would still be flooded but if the sunshine lasted all day they could move the livestock outside. If they moved the rabbits out of the brewery then Jacob would go as well and while that meant she wouldn't see him as often there was more of a chance of meeting, perhaps now in the secret cottage. She admonished herself for desire.

On her way to the kitchen, though, she stopped abruptly in the middle of the hall. A stop in the rain meant that the roads would soon be passable, and her identity was more likely to be challenged. Again. With the salon turned into a greenhouse and animals in the home there would be no escaping the conclusion that she was not a baroness. The cut of her dress wouldn't matter then. What would happen to her clan?

She pivoted and returned to the library where she paced the floor. Claudia came in with a radiant smile.

"The barley in the back acreage survived the rain. Even the hail! A whole group is going to harvest it. Mostly to be out of the house, I think! Imagine! Bread! Are you coming?"

"No, you go ahead. I'll…alert the baker."

As she slowly walked the hallway, the maids laughed and skipped toward the door. She caught the oldest maid by the arm.

"Check that the door in the back garden fence can be opened," she ordered. *We will need it when we flee.*

MT found Merek slowly raking the coals in the Garden Room fireplace.

"A good day to be a baker," she said, and he whirled around, stiffened and bowed his head.

"Milady."

"No more drying grass! And you must be pleased to hear of barley. A chance to bake."

His reaction was more subdued than she expected. "The mill is inoperable so... we have no way to grind it into flour."

"I see," MT said, puzzled, and returned to the library.

More important than bread, though, the day of reckoning was approaching, no doubt. The marchioness would talk, or the sheriff would return. Simon will have betrayed her, most certainly. MT would be hung or worse. Claudia would be killed as an accomplice, Daisy as well if they were cruel. Clearly they were cruel, or they would not have devised a scheme involving kidnap. The safety of her clan was of utmost importance. Not even the gold mattered. She stopped her pacing, startled. She had been so wrapped up in running her colony that for months she hadn't thought of fleeing with the gold. She wished she could give the gold to the servants: they would make better use of it than any royalty who descended on the place. And she couldn't bring herself to take it all and leave the servants penniless, homeless, and duped. But if she pressed a coin into each of their hands they could be strung up for theft, like the poor woman with the rabbit pelts.

What she tried not to dwell on, though, was that her life as head of a community was over. It had been the best thing that had ever happened to her, without a doubt. Even the loneliness of being separated from others couldn't dampen the feeling that this was her calling. Having done it, she was a different woman. Not just because of her lovemaking with Jacob, but because she knew she could never go back to the narrow life on her knees polishing wood and burning sage. Was the small taste of that better life gone now? The only question that remained was how to make sure that everyone left better off than when they had arrived. Right now, they were so excited about the barley. Maybe helping solve the milling problem was one last thing she could do.

The mill at the river's edge was the property of the bishop and she had already denied the bishop women for his brothel. Perhaps it was best to not trespass on him again. Besides, it was too large, too difficult and noisy for a simple, one-time grind of barley. *What about the millstones in the floor of the chapel?* she thought and threw on her cape to investigate.

When MT forced open the swollen door of the chapel and stepped into the gloom, she shrieked. Baudwin the sheriff was on his knees in front of the altar, so thin that his protruding shoulder blades resembled chicken wings. The drooping skin on his face, usually grey and pallid, was now deathly transparent and made his wide eyes seem like the only part of him left alive. She rushed to his side and found walnut shells on the floor and jerky in his saddle bag.

"Mother of God, man! Have you been here this whole time?" She looked at a high-water mark on the wall where it had flooded, the millstones that had nearly been chiseled from the floor, and a collection of fern bears covered with mold.

"Since the tent...for penance," he said weakly. "Are you here to pray with me?"

"No, we're looking for millstones," she said and tried to get him to stand but the difference in their height made it impossible.

MT took off her cape and covered Baudwin's back with it. "I'll return with food."

Instead, she sent two maids with a parcel of baked rabbit and apples with a beaker of broth, plus three hammers and a crowbar. They set the food on a bench, refusing to feed the man who had imprisoned them, and one maid spat at him when his back was turned. But they needed the stones, and their hammer blows were sharp like their anger. Baudwin, however, set aside his food and grabbed the crowbar, keeping pace with their hammering despite his depleted health. After several hours, they were able to extract two intact stones, and tucking them under their arms, they begrudgingly supported Baudwin between them as they walked him and the millstones back to the manor house.

That night MT heard muttering from the sheriff's room and discovered him feverish and shaking. Rousing several of the maids, they wrapped him in any spare blanket they could find, though they were still skittish with memories of the emaciated woman dead and buried without ceremony. MT smudged the doorframe with sage and when Gertrude set a bowl of broth on a sideboard in the hallway, unwilling to get any closer, MT took it in and tried to spoon it into his mouth. In the early hours he started wheezing and by daybreak he had died. Percy and the young boy dug a grave but only half the staff attended the quick and quiet funeral.

CHAPTER SIXTEEN

The end of the rain drove everyone, everywhere, outside. Villagers throughout East Anglia raised their faces to the sun, surprised at its warmth and then suddenly aware of how damp and mildewed their clothing had become, how fresh the air was and how fetid their armpits and pants.

A peasant swung his shepherding stick like a fancy cane and, whistling again now that man and beast were not trapped inside, drove his pigs back into the forest. Already feeling lucky to have survived the rains, he saw something sparkling in the undergrowth. Gold, he wondered. Jewels? He poked at the ground, then jumped back at his discovery. It was a skull in a white cap that was embroidered with shards of mirrors sewn into a scene of lions killing a stag, the third of the three caps of the baroness, the one she had been wearing when she died. The skull and cap had been carried so far by the flooding that no one had ever seen it or known the baroness. The curious sows began snuffling the ground and the peasant pushed them aside (since pigs, like goats, will eat anything, including valuable items that don't belong inside a pig.) Besides, wasn't that gold thread?

The cap was surprisingly clean and white, as if untouched by the decrepitude and rot that had taken the skull. Perhaps a wolf had taken the head off the body, carried it until it realized that it wasn't food, because the peasant couldn't find a body nearby, no man of finery or lady-in-waiting. The peasant put the tip of his stick through the eye socket, picked it up, and the newly emerged sunshine, so coveted itself, radiated off this golden and mirrored skull like an angel's touch.

Looking at it, the peasant felt lifted off the ground, cleansed, as if its glinting light had erased the scars on his hands and straightened the defeated slump of his shoulders. Here was something he had always wanted: a coveted possession, a reason for maids to flock to him and men to curtly bow their heads. He resolved to gather his pigs later, and he hurried to the market in town, where the cap sparkled amid the turnips and twig brooms. He cut through crowds with it in his hands; people pushed others aside to see what he had, and for the first time in his life he was remarkable, unique, lucky but also a little capable to have found it, wasn't he? Smart enough to now acknowledge what had to be its wonderous power, and whenever he could gather an audience, he embellished the story of its discovery: he had seen it in a dream not in a cluster of pigs, and he had been drawn to it by its mysterious force, not because he seized on anything shiny like a magpie.

He kept it in a sack, then a wooden box that an old man

gave him after proclaiming the skull so much more deserving than the threadbare heirlooms of his grandmother. The rag the peasant covered it with was replaced by a finely woven scarf. His standing improved, as women gave him a spiced bun or a whole boiled chicken for a chance to touch it. He was welcomed in every hamlet he approached. He was fed, given clothing better than anything that had ever touched his skin. He walked with a purpose, an identity, a destination.

The skull was carried on a pole in parades orchestrated to show gratitude for the long-awaited sunshine. Surely it belonged to a saint, since its miraculous fabric was unblemished and whiter than the bone it rode on, and soon the skull and cap were carried on a pillow in hastily organized religious processions. It blessed newborns with a sparkling future; it showed the old and dying the pearly gates; it drove the guilty to their knees in penance and those who tried to pick the gold thread from it when the peasant fell asleep drunk saw little bits of themselves being torn apart in Hell and they ran off.

There was no one on the peasant's journey who had ever seen the short and oddly shaped baroness, known of her wickedness, or the revelatory quality of her headgear until one day a week after the break in the rain he was in a market that was held outside the castle of the earl. He had never been there before, and he had expected the same welcome he had received in the villages *en route*. Instead, he was given a spot in the market between the tanner and the butcher. It enraged him: didn't they know what he had? Didn't they know who he was? The stench of blood and urine made him woozy, so he was a bit off balance when a scullery maid trying to flee from the earl's castle with two silver spoons in her pocket stopped in her tracks at the sight of it. She couldn't remember when it had appeared or who had been wearing it, but it had been seen at one of the countess's banquets, she was sure. The kitchen had been abuzz with tales of the gloom and sorrow it reflected, despite the summer sunshine and the rare fruits on the menu at the time.

Neither the maid nor the peasant would ever recall the conversation that ensued but would remember just before falling asleep every night thereafter, the sight of her hand giving over the spoons and the peasant relinquishing the box and skull. She dreamt of a shrewd transaction, royalty singing of her loyal and cunning nature, a dramatic invitation to the high table and the gift of a flowing dress. Then she descended into a nightmare of scrubbing a never-ending hallway while a black crow drew blood from her shoulder and demanded to know how she had acquired this scull. The peasant dreamt of shaking the silver spoons at an auction and winning a flock and a herd, but it turned into the nightmare of being lost in a crowd while a thief picked his pocket just before the sheriff cut off his hands.

That day, though, the scullery maid hurried back to the castle with the box and waved away questions of where she had been. With authority, she set the box on the kitchen worktable amid plucked chickens and cleavers but when she lifted the lid and the cloth, pandemonium ensued. News of the box's arrival spread through the castle and there was a steady stream of servants and staff pouring into the kitchen all day.

At first people turned away from the skull but then leaned in for closer examination. In the reflections on the cap, the cook saw herself cut up and put into a stew. The chief chamber maid saw little reenactments of her dalliance with the teenage boys of the gentry. The keeper of the larder saw the sins that had brought on the rain. The head of the armory looked in and left with his hands covering his weeping face. Only the baker's lass saw a spring day, herself young and fresh, smiling at a gentle life.

The moment that the earl and countess heard of the cap and its skull the earl slammed his fists on the table and stood.

The countess laid her hand on his forearm and tried to settle him. "It cannot be her. Mother dined there before the rains, didn't you?" She turned to the aged and stooped marchioness, who grunted in agreement but offered no further details.

The earl commanded that the box be brought to him but when the lid was opened, he turned from the grizzled vision of himself in the little mirrors.

"Look at this, woman," he commanded his wife. "Is this not your friend, the baroness?"

"Oh, I dare not, milord," the countess said, remembering the wicked circus that had crawled over the baroness's head when she had visited them before the Great Mortality. She had assigned the sour-tongued woman a seat as far away from herself as she could and still was certain that the cap had broadcast to her husband the faces of the lute player she had been entertaining late at night. "Mother," she pleaded, "you look."

The marchioness, who vacillated between pity and disgust that her daughter had married beneath her and to a brutish man at that, struggled to her feet. With dramatic, editorial stabs of her cane against the flagstone, she shuffled forward and looked into the box. "I knew there was something wrong," she muttered. "The clothing fit her; she looked like a turnip as always. There couldn't be two, I told myself," as she remembered the dark and painful images of her own death that she had seen in the black cap. "But there was something off."

"What was that, Mother?"

"The staff was almost…jovial."

"Jovial?" the earl bellowed. "The woman had a heart of bog mud!" He paced behind the high table. "So, an imposter is in the barony, playing me for a fool." He looked into the box again and saw a jester's cap on his own visage. "No wonder she wouldn't send the peasants to me." He summoned his chief of staff. "We ride to the manor as soon as the roads are clear! Find an executioner and be sure he rides with us. Blade sharpened."

His staff turned to leave.

"And tell no one! Do you hear?" He pointed to everyone in the banquet hall. "I want to catch her in the act."

Though the staff dutifully kept news of the imposter a secret, the search for the executioner alerted all the surrounding villages and word got back to the manor house that the earl was going to dispense a wicked justice somewhere, soon.

~ * ~ * ~ * ~

Hearing of the executioner and the earl, Claudia and MT paced the floor of the library with agitation.

"Why are we still here?" Claudia demanded.

"Because we haven't devised a way to take everyone with us. If they're bringing the executioner, more than one head will roll."

"You saved their lives. Perhaps you've done enough."

MT ducked under the desk, hit the lever and dragged the bag of gold into the middle of the room. Claudia gasped as she had when she first saw it, and she checked the lock on the door.

"What will you do?" MT asked her.

Claudia was fixated on the bag. "I don't know," she said absently. "Go off with my children of course."

MT looked at her darkly yet couldn't bring herself to ask about either the death of the starving woman or the coldness toward Percy that seemed to have settled in her friend.

MT dug into the bag of gold and pressed a handful of coins into Claudia's hands, who sighed and tucked them into her pockets. "Take Percy with you, then. Start a farm."

"No," Claudia said. "He is staying nearby so the risk of Daisy's discovery is too great...if she's short...or a distant relative...or even a royal sees the similarity. Besides, he would want children of his own, which I can't do."

MT smiled sadly and gripped her arm. "I would give a coin to each of the staff here, but they would be accused of theft."

"If you do give them a coin, it should be hidden, even from them, until they are far away from the manor," Claudia said.

"Still, even years from now they would be accused if they used them."

"Not if they had permission. Something stating their permission."

"None of them can read! Nor anyone in the market or trades."

MT pondered their situation. Then she paced quickly to the desk and rifled through the drawers. She pulled out the stamp of the baron and waved it triumphantly. Claudia nodded. The two continued to pace.

"Something precious, that they will treasure, that can hide the coin."

"At this point the most precious thing is bread," Claudia joked, and started another lap around the room.

"Buns. Individual barley buns. Put the coin in before it bakes..." MT said.

"Presented in a little bit of cloth...tied with a string..."

"With a stamped tag that says "With gratitude for...""

"No. Gratitude will mark it as a forgery for sure."

MT straightened her shoulders, lifted her chin and waved her hand around to imagine what a royal would say. "For services rendered," she said with a haughty tone.

"Exactly. Now start writing and stamping," Claudia said. "I'll check with the baker." She looked outside at the sunshine. "No time to lose."

Merek watched them grinding the barley between the small millstones. When they turned to him for guidance, he gave a noncommittal nod of his head. It was bound to be coarser than wheat flour, anyone would know that, and he just had to guess. He ran it through his hands, and then wheeled the single small barrel of it into the kitchen where they had resumed the fire. His cheeks were flushed, the knot so tight in his chest that his breath was shallow. He was so tired of hiding his secret that he wanted to blurt it out and be done with it. Instead, he spoke to Gertrude in half-sentences.

"The bakery...and all the grass. I can't..."

"Yes," she said. "Let's make the dough here in the kitchen, if you don't mind my butting in."

"Don't mind at all." He had wanted to share the story with Gertrude but reflexively dodged the truth again.

She pushed back her sleeves and Merek decided that rather than ducking out of the room to hide, as he usually did, he would stand at her elbow. What he learned shocked him. A nest of barley flour. An egg cracked in the middle. A splash of milk. The arms of a strong woman mixing and kneading.

"Do you find it better to whip the egg before adding it?" she asked him.

"I like the way you do it." He rolled up his shirtsleeves and copied her actions. The tenuous relief of making the bread fought with a renewed rage at his mother that something so simple would have been hidden from her own family. Flour, egg, a splash of milk. Why had that been too much to share? But more importantly, why, in all the years of his travels, had he not just asked how it was done? True, the villagers arrived with their dough ball already shaped and proofed but the whole process turned out to be so basic. Why hadn't he learned something so simple on his own? Why had he resigned himself to his deficiency and then clung so tightly to the secret of it? Clung to his rage? Was it pride? Disbelief that he could have what he wanted?

"I can't…knead it like that," he said, chagrined.

"Pick it up on the end and slap it down," Gertrude said, and smiled but before she could turn back to her dough, he covered her hand with his and leaned close to her ear. He spilled out his story, his parents' death, the stalling tactics of his tall tales, the paucity of his knowledge, his endless fury at his mother, his ignorance and shame. The more he talked the more his legs grew weak until the two were sitting on a bench, still holding hands. The fire-side stories he told made him no better than a puppet in a market, he lamented. A person who made nothing. A man without purpose.

"No! Not true. We didn't know of Prester John before you. Or the truth of the Far East. Tennis! You make us see. As important as a loaf of barley bread! And your fires are commendable. An even burn is not easy to achieve."

Claudia strode into the kitchen with urgent purpose. "Oh good, you've started." The two stood quickly and dropped hands. "The baroness would like them baked into individual buns. And she would like to inspect them before they go into the oven."

When Claudia returned to the library, MT was sitting at her desk behind little stacks of coins and tags.

"Even giving them two there's so much left over," MT said. "I'd rather burn it or bury it or throw it into the river rather than leave it for the earl."

Claudia nodded her agreement. "Take the rest with you."

"I have no desire to live as a rich woman." MT was forlorn, slumped in her chair.

"That's not the problem, is it," Claudia stated.

MT sighed. "I have loved this, Claudia. Now I have nowhere to go, no community at all."

"You could start a hospital."

"I don't know anything about medicine."

"Give it to the Church."

"Not in a million years!"

"Open stables. A delivery service. A farm."

"Yes, I'll give more to Percy."

"Why not a school?" Claudia said.

"No, the church controls them. And they won't take girls." She looked at her friend with her insatiable desire for children. "How about an orphanage?" She sat forward, more convinced of this idea's worth. "I'll give the gold to you. For more babies than you can imagine." She carefully studied Claudia's face for any clues to the hungry woman's death.

"An orphanage!" Surrounded by children. Rescuing children, as she hadn't been able to do during the plague. The childless mother and the motherless children. A weight lifted off Claudia's shoulders. No explanations necessary. Orphans. She beamed back at her friend. "And you? Where will you go?"

Someplace where I can play like I had with Jacob, MT thought, but shrugged.

The two pondered the ideas while inspecting the tags and their seals that MT had made with candle wax mixed with soot from the fireplace.

"These look good," Claudia said.

MT approached her next topic with trepidation. "What about Jacob?" Though it was a relationship built on false pretenses because he didn't seem to notice that she wasn't the real baroness, it was also made of vulnerability and genuine feelings, MT thought, and she didn't want to leave without him. But what right did she have? "He is Daisy's father, after all." What she didn't say was that no one had ever been as dear to her as Jacob and the thought of riding him made her blush. MT gulped and gathered her courage. "If he'll go with me, may I take Jacob along?"

"Oh, that would ease my heart, MT. And if he's with you I will know that he will be cared for."

The two women clasped hands. "Thank you," Claudia whispered, "for saving me." MT kissed their joined knuckles.

There was a knock on the door. They both flinched and though they knew it was locked, Claudia rushed to it and put her palm against it. "Yes?"

"Milady asked to inspect the buns. They're ready for the oven. And the oven in the bakery is hot."

"Thank you. She'll be along directly."

They bagged the gold and MT held one in each hand under her cloak. "Should we tell everyone?" she asked Claudia.

"No! The less they know the safer they are."

MT nodded and walked to the bakery.

MT looked odd in her cloak as she entered the hot bakery. "Lovely work," she said to Merek and Gertrude. "But I need your assistance... your involvement... in a very important task." She set the partial bags of gold down with a thud.

MT considered. She didn't need to reveal her charade. The next steps would be challenging enough.

"We all have to leave here. Danger is on its way. But I want everyone to leave with… something to set them up. As a token of my appreciation." She bent down and brought out a handful of gold coins.

The two were shocked, both by the quantity of gold and her willingness to share it.

"Two coins into each bun. They mustn't know they're in there until they're far away from here."

There was a quiet knock at the door. MT let Claudia in, and she brought a large piece of wool that hid the stamped tags.

"Have they agreed?" Claudia asked her.

"With great pleasure, milady," said Merek. Gertrude curtsied, still stunned.

"Right. Let's begin."

The four of them stuffed and baked, wrapped and tagged the buns. Watching the rolls bake as he leaned on his tall peel, Merek realized that he had always wanted to bake something sublime but now he was baking something that would change a life.

MT pressed four coins and a tag into Merek's hands, then Gertrude's. "You will leave in the morning. We all will."

Merek bent over their clasped hands. "Where will you go, milady?"

MT took off the cap, scratched her hair and smiled at him,

a disarming smile on an ordinary face. "No idea. But Claudia is going to build a home for orphans."

Merek looked at her with greater consideration than he ever had. "So, I was right, you're not a royal, are you?"

"No."

"And yet the portrait…and the clothing," Gertrude said carefully, still tentative in speaking to her, as if somehow, somewhere she might still retain power. And unsure of how she felt about the oddity of a woman who wasn't royal, but wealthy, and generous.

MT shrugged her shoulders and turned her palms up. There was no explaining it.

When MT left, Merek turned back to Gertrude. "Perhaps together," he said haltingly. "A baker and a cook."

She looked down shyly but stepped closer to him. "Motherless children are certainly people who matter."

That night MT stood at the head of the high table that had been pressed back into service after the rains stopped. She wore the cap for the last time. She looked at each of the expectant faces, at Claudia, the babies strapped to her and the orphans at her side, at Percy and Jacob, Merek and Gertrude, the lovely young maids from the cart, the old man and orphan sentry.

They had been in the house little more than two weeks before the rains came and had spent three months here out of the deluge. She cleared her throat.

"While we are all so grateful to have survived the rain,

there is another danger on its way, and we must all leave this place in the morning." The youngest girls gasped and looked at each other, instantly afraid. "Without exception, we must all leave. Tonight, pack your things in one of the rucksacks, say your goodbyes, and in the morning I will give each of you a gift to help you on your way. Get as far away as you can, and it might be better to not discuss with others your time here. Ever." She looked back at Claudia, who nodded curtly. MT wanted to thank them but was afraid she would break down and cry. If she looked over at Jacob she would weep, she knew.

After dinner, Percy seized Claudia's wrist as she tried to slip past him in the hallway. "So, we're all to leave," he said.

"Where will you go?" she asked without meeting his gaze.

"This farm will just flood again so I'm going back west to a farm by the road. I had bad luck with a grifter there but I'm wiser now."

She nodded but looked at the floor.

"I was hoping…you might join me. As my wife."

Claudia stepped back. The farm was too close to the manor. There were children who needed her. She shook her head.

"So, the rumor of an orphanage is true."

"Yes."

Percy sighed forlornly and shuffled his feet. He wasn't sure he could do it without her. Or that he wanted to. *Inevitable, though, that the dog-boy would be rebuffed.* "You should take the cow and calf with you, then."

As soon as the sun was up enough to send the wolves to their dens, the staff of the manor began leaving, though a dense fog obliterated the horizon just past the beginning of the fields. MT stood at the back door of the gate, in the baroness's most simple dress and her boots, without a cap but in a cloud of sage smoke that each would walk through. She marveled that everyone here had been delivered from the rain, protected from the flood, and had had food while others starved. Better than that, everyone here had gotten what they had always wanted. Claudia was a mother, though through suspicious means, perhaps. Percy was a farmer, despite his self-doubt. All the maids had been freed from a life of imprisonment. Merek had abandoned his resentment and become a baker. Gertrude had realized that there's more to riches than the show of wealth. As for herself, she had had a chance to not only play like a child and experience passion for the first time, but to love people through her ideas; to love them with order, structure and care. The only failures were Simon who kept running and poor Baudwin who had died of guilt.

She pressed a little pouch into each of their hands, made sure the women were traveling together in a small group and was heartened to see that Gertrude had given each of the women a sharp knife from the kitchen or a larger knife in a sheath. A few of the women tried to convince her to take them with her but she peeled their hands off her arm and declined, sputtering excuses in half-sentences. She stroked their cheeks, their hair, asked about warm clothing and if they had family or a plan for their destination.

MT smiled when she saw that Merek and Gertrude were arm in arm, lit up with the possibilities. "Together, your pies will be outstanding!"

"Milady," Merek said. "Pies for Claudia's children."

MT choked on her words. "Those would be most welcome, I'm sure."

The quiet staff walked an erratic line on the path but were soon swallowed by the fog. Percy drove a wagon beside the manor wall, crates of chickens and farm tools in the back, the elkhound beside him, and the young orphan boy herding the sheep with the help of the other dogs. The fighting dogs would not leave Jacob, so Percy relinquished them and while Jacob didn't understand the gift, he took comfort in the dogs' devotion. Claudia had presented Percy with four barley buns that she said were a special gift from the baroness and he kept them in a clay urn at his feet to keep the dogs out of them. He drove away with farming knowledge from Claudia, though not her love.

Behind him was Claudia's wagon, with two beds, four children, pots and pans and a substantial amount of gold hidden in her dress, under the seat, in the bedding, under a false bottom in a basket of eggs and in another basket of dried fish. The cow was tied to the rail with the calf at her side and the old man was perched on the end of the wagon swinging his legs, grinning at Merek and Gertrude, who were bright-eyed and quick-stepped behind them. The wagon stopped and Claudia, with both babies strapped to her chest, held MT's outstretched hands.

"The starving woman...the children's mother...she was

dead when I came in that morning," Claudia said quietly. "The look on her face…so horrified. I couldn't let the children see her like that."

MT closed her eyes and sighed with relief. *Would you have*, she wanted to ask but didn't.

"Come with me," Claudia said. "You run the foundling home; I'll care for the children."

MT was unsure. "What road are you taking?"

"Toward York."

MT nodded her head. "York. Good. Is that everyone?"

"That's everyone."

"Where is Jacob?" MT looked across the garden. "Have you seen him?" MT started to panic. "Where is Jacob?"

Claudia sputtered her surprise. "I haven't seen him this morning. Are his rabbits in the…"

"Go!" MT ordered her. "You're slow moving and…need the time. I'll handle this."

"But they're looking for you, MT."

"I can't leave him. What if they question him and… I can't leave him." *And don't want to leave him*, she thought.

"Walk on!" Claudia ordered the horse but turned in her seat. "Bring him with you!"

MT ran to the brewery but was not surprised to see that there were no rabbits, baskets or cages. *He's returned to the warren lodge*, she thought, and then imagined the executioner that was heading their way. She had to leave, but she ran to the library and got the bag containing the remainder of the gold, grabbed the bearskin pelt and ran through the deserted manor, past the stripped garden toward the lodge.

When she arrived, breathless, MT dropped the sack by the door, shuffled through the rabbits that had colonized the first floor, then she took the stairs two at a time despite her short legs. The fighting dogs had positioned themselves in the corner of the room. When she found Jacob crouching between the bed and the wall, holding Julia to his chest, she fell on her knees and put her hands on his shoulders.

"Come with me," she pleaded. He shook his head and looked away.

"Please. Bring Julia but come with me."

He raised his eyes. "Don't go."

MT thought about it: settling in here as the wife of the warrener, but she quickly set those ideas aside. Her physical stature, which had convinced everyone of her lineage, would reveal her, without a doubt.

"We'll start again. Another warren. Made of your favorites. With Claudia and many children."

He sat up straighter.

"We'll have bunnies and a garden. We can ride," she said a bit sheepishly, unaccustomed to acknowledging her desire. "And laugh. And be together." She could have that life, couldn't she? One that included both fun and responsibility. She stood and took his hand, guiding him up. She picked two of the rabbits in dresses, ran downstairs and put them into cages. "Quickly now," she called up to him, and they filled the cages and baskets, then put the sack in the cart. Jacob spoke in a low voice to each rabbit as he dropped them into a cage, took the cage of the largest buck from a table and admonished it. She harnessed the fighting dogs to the front bar of the cart, covered the cart with the bearskin and they both stepped under the awning.

"We shall be safe now, Baroness," Jacob said.

"Call me Mary."

"Safe now, Baroness Mary, now that *I* am the bear."

~ * ~ * ~ * ~

The earl and his entourage seemed to emerge from the ground as they charged through the fog to the open gates of the manor. The earl dismounted, grabbed the incriminating box of skull and cap from his saddlebag and barged into the house. He slowed when he saw that the building was empty.

"Baroness!" he called, his voice ringing off the walls. "Imposter! Show yourself!"

Undaunted, he strode to the library where he saw the portrait, the mirror and the three wall-mounted hat stands, one of which was empty, all hung at the level of his chest. A black one. A white one. An empty spot for the one in his box.

"Your Grace," his first-in-command called. "You'll want to see this."

The earl's rage increased with each room he entered. He growled over rabbit pellets in the brewery and chicken feathers in the laundry. He shrieked over the forbidden millstones and predicted the bishop's rage. Finally, he howled over the indignity of beans growing up the Grecian columns, the soil rotting the fine wooden floors, the denuded vines of squash snaking around dirt-filled beds where the gentry had once slept.

The sergeant-at-arms, however, who had witnessed the shrinking of his underfed squad and the desperation of hungry villagers who had come to the earl's gates only to be turned away, smiled to himself at the ingenuity of an indoor farm. Stroking his beard, and looking out the window, the horizon caught his eye, and for years afterward, in telling the tale of the story-telling cap and misplaced skull, the cruel baroness and the odd imposter, he insisted that he saw a bear lumbering near the warren lodge, headed for the woods.

ABOUT THE AUTHOR

Website: www.jesswells.com
Wikipedia: https://en.wikipedia.org/wiki/Jess_Wells
Facebook: https://www.facebook.com/JessWellsAuthor/
Amazon Author Page

Jess Wells is the author of seven novels and five books of short stories, as well as the editor of anthologies of social commentary. She is the winner of the Nautilus Silver Prize for Small Press Fiction with a Social Impact, Bronze Winner of the Foreword Indies Awards, a four-time finalist for the national Lambda Literary Awards, a member of the Saints and Sinners Literary Festival Hall of Fame, and a recipient of a San Francisco Arts Commission Grant for Literature. Her books are sold through all online distributors and her audio books can be found on Spotify, iTunes, and Audible, among other locations. Her work has been included in more than three dozen anthologies and literary journals, reprinted in the United Kingdom and translated into Italian and Dutch. She has taught at literary conferences and teaching locations across the U.S. Visit her website at www.jesswells.com or her Wikipedia page at https://en.wikipedia.org/wiki/Jess_Wells.

DISCUSSION GUIDE

1. Describe your reaction when you finally got something that you have always wanted. Was it different than the reaction you thought you would have?

2. Discuss the desires of each character and what they realized when they got what they wanted.

   a. MT wanted room for her ideas and leadership skills, only to discover that it's lonely at the top.

   b. Claudia wanted a child but became insatiable and willing to do almost anything to get one.

   c. Simon wanted absolution by the ghost of the soldier boy, but the torment had consumed so much of his life that the void was more terrifying than the torment. He refused what he wanted.

   d. Merek wanted skills that had been kept from him but realized that he had spent a lifetime on his anger and pride instead of learning the simple tasks.

   e. Gertrude wanted to cook for royalty but discovered that other people matter as much.

3. Whose struggle can you identify with most?

4. Compare the quiet in the world after the first wave of the plague and what you experienced during the Covid-19 pandemic of 2020.

5. Did you know anything about rabbit farming before reading the book? Baking in the Medieval world?

www.ingramcontent.com/pod-product-compliance
Lightning Source LLC
Chambersburg PA
CBHW010812250626
47169CB00009B/2912